Mini Wonderful Curves

16 Seasonal Quilt Projects Using the QCR Mini

by Jenny Pedigo and Helen Robinson
for Sew Kind of Wonderful
with Sherilyn Mortensen

Landauer Publishing

Mini Wonderful Curves
16 Seasonal Quilt Projects Using the QCR Mini

Landauer Publishing, *www.landauerpub.com*, is an imprint of Fox Chapel Publishing Company, Inc.

Editor/Art Director: Laurel Albright
Editor/Photographer: Sue Voegtlin

Library of Congress Control Number: 2017963441

ISBN: 978-1-935726-99-9

We are always looking for talented authors.
To submit an idea, please send a brief inquiry to acquisitions@foxchapelpublishing.com.

Printed in China

Eighth printing

Introduction

"Before Sew Kind of Wonderful we were three sisters busy sewing, creating, working, cooking, mothering, taxiing, serving, and crafting. We were trying to beautify our homes, share with our friends and families and make our little corner of the world just a little bit 'cuter.' One of our favorite types of quilts to create were seasonal quilts. These gorgeous little gems would make their appearance for a month or two and then get switched out for the next fun little diddy that just magically was sewn up over the weekend!

Jenny

Well, we still love seasonal quilts and wanted to explore a whole year's worth of seasonal quilts with the QCR Mini Ruler. We wanted to use the same basic 'wonderful' curved block which we used in 'One Wonderful Curve' as the foundation for each of these quilts just on a smaller scale. We brainstormed some fun seasonal quilt ideas and bought fabric (yeah!) in January 2017. Off we each went to our little corners of paradise and cut and sewed and texted pictures back and forth and sewed some more and quilted a bunch and "poof" 4 months later we had sixteen fantastic seasonal quilts. No big deal!

Helen

We are so excited to share these quick and easy weekend projects that we had so much fun creating!"

Sherilyn

Jenny, Helen, and Sherilyn

You will need the QCR Mini Ruler to complete the projects in this book.

Look for the QCR Mini© at your favorite quilt shop or
visit Sewkindofwonderful.com for ordering information and ruler tutorials.

Contents

Contents

Techniques QCR Mini Ruler© (QCRM)

CUTTING THE CURVES

Each project in the book uses the same basic curved shape. We suggest you practice cutting and piecing the curves using the steps provided before beginning a project.

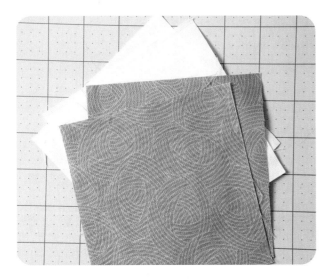

1. Stack (1) 5" x 5" fabric square and (1) 5" x 5" contrasting fabric square. This will give you enough pieces to practice making two blocks.

Note: When making several blocks for a project, you can stack a few pieces, right sides up, for cutting.

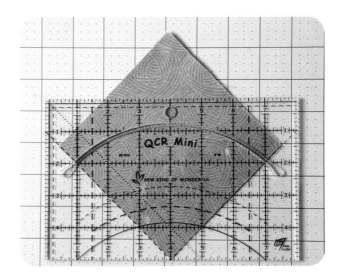

2. Align the adjoining sides along the dashed "V" lines on the QCRM ruler.

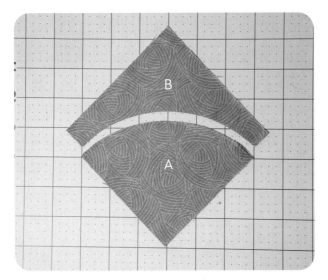

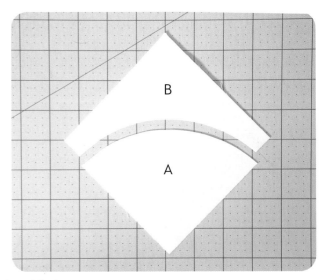

3. Using a 45mm rotary cutter, cut in the curved cutout to make A and B shapes.

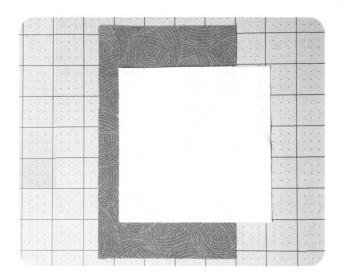

1. Cut (1) 4-½" x 7-½" fabric rectangle and (1) 5-½" contrasting fabric square. This will give you enough pieces to practice making two blocks.

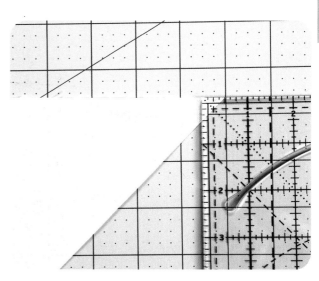

2. Cut the 5-½" contrasting fabric square in half diagonally. Measure in ½" on each point and trim.

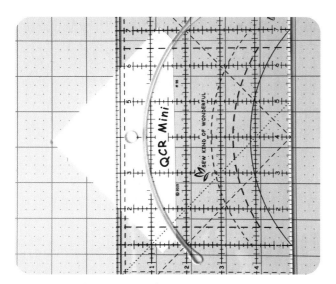

3. Position the QCR on the triangle with the curved cutout over the points as shown.

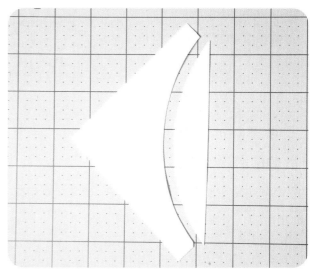

4. Using a 45mm rotary cutter, cut in the ruler's curved cutout to make a B shape. Discard the small piece.

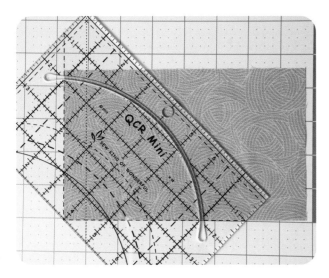

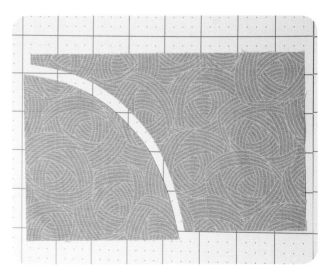

5. Place the 4-1/2" x 7-1/2" fabric rectangle right side up on a cutting surface. Position the QCR Mini Ruler on the rectangle aligning the adjoining sides along the dashed "V" lines on the ruler.

6. Using a rotary cutter cut in the curved cutout to make an A shape.

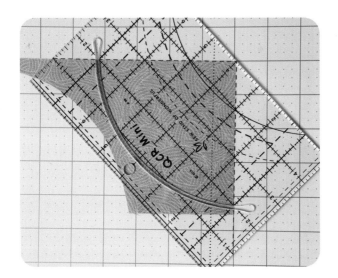

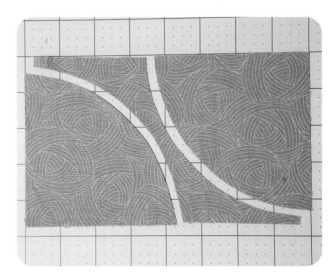

7. Position the QCR Mini ruler on the opposite corner and cut to make an additional A shape. Discard the small center piece.

TIP: Do not stack more than four fabric pieces when cutting.

Techniques QCR Mini Ruler© (QCRM)

PIECING THE CURVES

The curves will be pieced in the same manner in each project. Always use a ¼" seam and sew with right sides together.

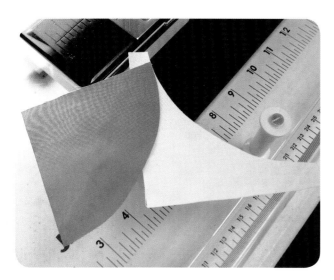

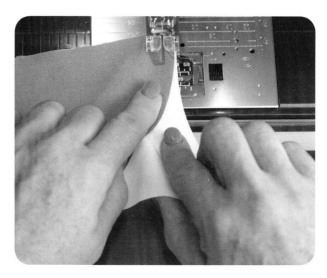

1. Position an A shape on a B shape, right sides together, with ½" of B extending beyond A.

2. Hold one shape in each hand and slowly bring the curved edges together while stitching a ¼" seam.

> TIP: When sewing the curves, try placing the outside curve (top piece) in your right hand and the inside curve (bottom piece) in your left hand. The curve comes together easily, but experiment to see what works best for you.

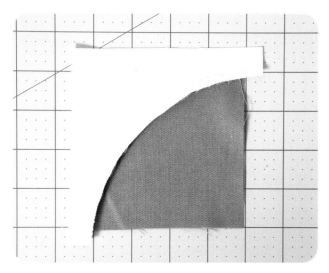

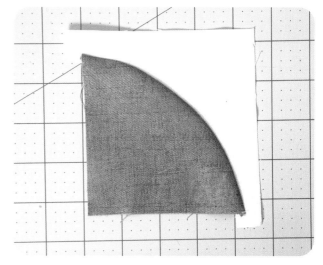

3. Press seam toward A to make an AB unit. Press the unit from the back and the front.

SQUARING UP THE UNITS

The Mini Curve Ruler has a 1/8" line to help align AB units when squaring up. We suggest you practice squaring up the units using the photos shown below to help with accurate cuts.

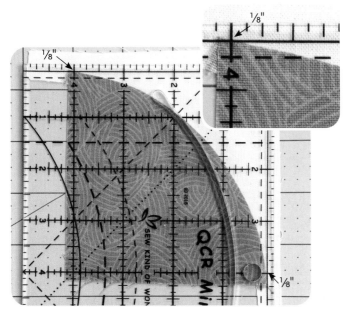

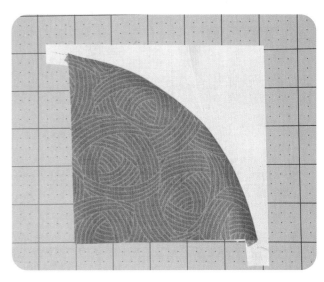

1. Square up the AB units to 4" x 4" square. Position QCR Mini on AB shape with the B part at the top right position. Leave an 1/8" from curved seam to outer edge, making sure that the 4" and 1/8" lines of the ruler intersect the seam line. (See inset)

2. Trim right side and top edge of the unit.

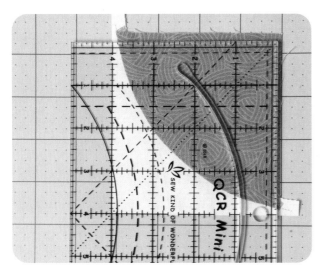

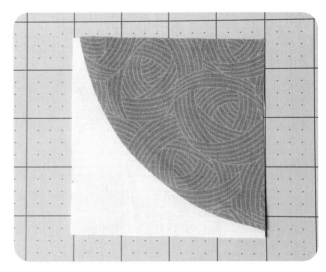

3. Lift ruler, rotate block, reposition QCR Mini aligning previously trimmed edges with the 4" marks.

4. Trim the right side and top edge to square up the unit.

And the day came when the risk to remain tight in a bud

was more painful than the risk it took to *blossom.*

—Anaïs Nin

Early Risers

FINISHED SIZE: 37" X 47"

MATERIALS

(6) 12" assorted print fabric squares for tulips
(6) 8" assorted solid fabric squares for tulip centers
(6) 12" assorted solid green fabric squares
     for leaves
2-1/2 yards background fabric
1-1/2 yards backing fabric
1/2 yard bind fabric
QCR Mini Ruler (QCRM)

GENERAL CUTTING INSTRUCTIONS

From *each* assorted print fabric square, cut:
(2) 4-1/2" x 7-1/2" pieces for tulips for a total of 12
(1) 1" x 4" piece for tulip centers for a total of 6

From *each* assorted solid fabric square, cut:
(1) 5-1/2" square for tulip center, for a total of 6
(1) 1" x 4" piece for tulip centers for a total of 6

From *each* assorted solid green fabric
square, cut:
(2) 5" squares for leaves for a total of 12
(1) 5-1/2" square for leaves. Cut in half diagonally
     for a total of 12 triangles
(1) 1" x 10" strip for stems for a total of 6

From background fabric, cut:
(1) 5-1/2" x WOF strip. From the strip, cut:
     (6) 5-1/2" squares for tulip centers
(3) 5" x WOF strips. From the strips, cut:
     (24) 5" squares
(7) 4" x WOF strips. From the strips, cut:
     (12) 4" x 71/2" pieces
     (6) 4" x 6-1/2" pieces
     (6) 4" squares
     (18) 3" x 4" pieces
(6) 2" x WOF strips. Sew strips end to end, and cut:
     (3) 2" x 43-1/2" strips
     (2) 2" x 38" strips

WOF = width of fabric
Read through Using the QCR Mini Ruler,
pages 6-10 before beginning this project.

CUTTING WITH THE QCR MINI RULER

1. From the (12) 4-1/2" x 7-1/2" assorted print fabrics, stack a few, and align the adjoining sides along the dashed "V" lines on the QCRM ruler. Using a rotary cutter cut in the curved cutout to make (12) A shapes. Repeat on the opposite diagonal corner. Keep shapes matched by color. Continue cutting all pieces to make a total of (24) A shapes for tulip petals. Discard small pieces of fabric. Evenly divide Tulip A shapes into Stack 1 and 2 with (2) of each color in stacks.

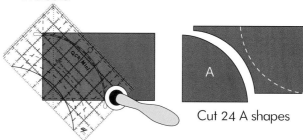

Cut 24 A shapes

2. From the (12) 5" assorted solid green fabric squares, stack a few, aligning the sides along the dashed "V" lines on the QCRM ruler. Cut in the curved cutout (red dashed line) to make (12) green A shapes and (12) green B shapes.

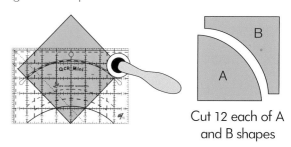

Cut 12 each of A
and B shapes

3. From the (12) green assorted triangles, stack a few, and measure and mark 1/2" on each diagonal point as shown.

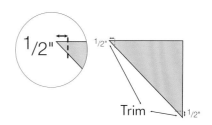

Trim

4. Position the QCRM ruler with curved cutout lays over points as shown. Cut in curved cutout to make (12) green B shapes. Discard small pieces of fabric

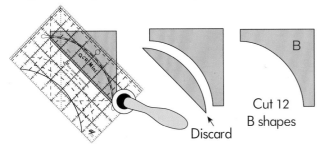

Cut 12 B shapes

Discard

5. From the (24) 5" background fabric squares, stack a few, aligning the sides along the dashed "V" lines on the QCRM ruler. Using a rotary cutter, cut in the curved cutout (red dashed line) to make (24) A shapes and (24) B shapes.

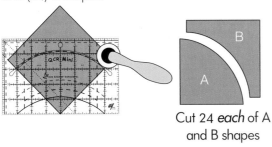

Cut 24 *each* of A and B shapes

PIECING THE CURVES

1. Using the matched color A shapes for tulip petals, from Stack 1 (page 13), position an assorted print A shape on a background B shape, right sides together, with B extending 1/2" beyond A.

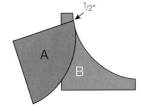

2. Hold one shape in each hand and slowly bring the curved edges together while stitching a 1/4" seam. Press seam toward A and press front and back of AB unit.

Press seam →

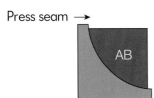

Make 12 print/background lower AB tulip units

3. Position a background A shape on a B assorted green shape, right sides together with B extending 1/2" beyond A.

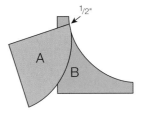

4. Referring to step 2, make 24 background/green assorted leaf AB units. Press seam toward A and press front and back of AB unit.

Press seam →

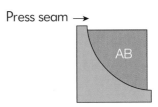

Make 24 background/green leaf units

5. Position an assorted green A shape on a background B shape, right sides together with B extending 1/2" beyond A.

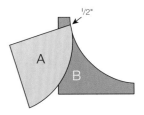

6. Referring to step 2, make (12) assorted green/ background AB leaf units. Press seam toward A and press front and back of AB unit.

Press seam →

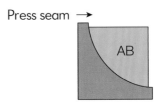

Make 12 green/background leaf units

SQUARING UP THE AB UNITS

Square up the AB units to 4" squares. Position the QCRM on AB unit as shown, with the B piece at the top right position. Leave ⅛" from curved seam to outer edges. Trim right side and top. Lift ruler, rotate block, reposition QCRM, aligning previously trimmed edges with the 4" marks on the ruler. Trim side and top. Repeat for all AB units.

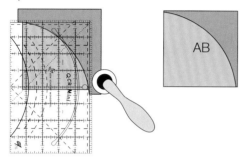

HALF-SQUARE TRIANGLE UNITS

1. Stack (1) 5-½" background square and (1) 5-½" assorted solid square, right sides together. Draw a diagonal line from corner to corner on wrong side of lighter fabric.

2. Sew ¼" on each side of the drawn line. Cut in half diagonally to make 2 background/assorted solid tulip center blocks. Press seam open.

3. Trim to make a 5" half-square triangle.

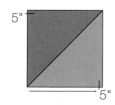

4. Repeat with remaining 5-½" background/assorted solid squares to make a total of (12) half-square triangle blocks.

5. Stack two half-square triangle blocks, right sides together, matching fabrics. Place QCRM on top of stacked unit and align adjoining sides under the dashed "V" line. Cut in the curved cutout to make (2) half-square B shapes.

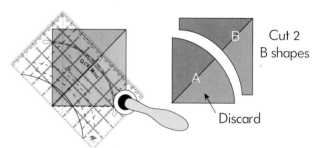

Cut 2
B shapes

Discard

6. Repeat for all half-square triangle blocks to make a total of (12) half–square B shapes. Press seams open.

NOTE: Save the A units for another project or discard.

MAKING THE BLOCKS
Tulip Tops

1. Pair the half-square B shapes with the print tulip A shapes as shown. Position print tulip A shapes on the half-square B shapes, right sides together, with B extending ½" beyond A.

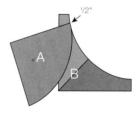

2. Hold one shape in each hand and slowly bring the curved edges together while stitching a ¼" seam. Press seams toward A. Press AB units on front and back.

Press seam →

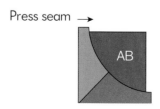

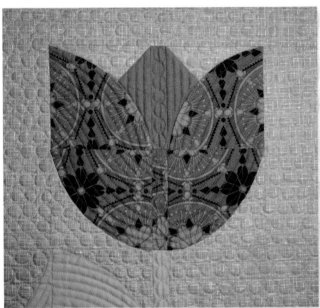

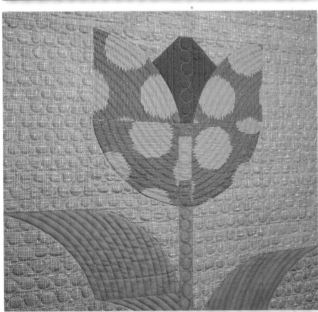

3. Square AB units to 4" squares. Try to align upper right hand corner of the ruler on seam of half-square B shape as close as possible.

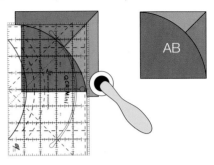

4. Sew a 1 x 4" tulip center to two sides of mirrored AB units as shown. Press seams open. Make (6) tulip top units.

  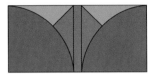

Make 6 tulip top units

Tulip Bottoms

Sew a 1" x 4" tulip center to two sides of mirrored AB units as shown. Press seams open. Make (6) tulip bottom units.

Make 6 tulip bottom units

Tulip Unit Assembly

Layout (2) 4" x 7-1/2" background pieces, 1 tulip top unit, and 1 tulip bottom unit as shown. Sew tulip top/bottom units together and sew a background piece to each side of the tulip. Make (6) tulip units. Press seams open to reduce bulk.

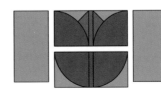 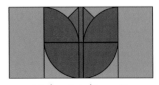

Make 6 tulip units

Tulip Leaves

Layout 4 background/solid green AB units, (2) solid green/background AB units, (1) 4" background square, (3) 3" x 4" background pieces (1) 4" x 6-1/2" background piece and (1) 1" x 10" solid green strip as shown. Sew unit together, pressing seams open to reduce bulk. Arrange pieces to make different leaf set arrangements as shown in Tulip Blocks graphic below. Make (6) tulip leaf units.

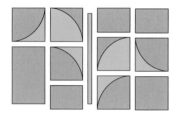 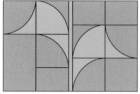

Make 6 tulip leaf units

Tulip Blocks

Lay out (6) tulip units and (6) leaf units and sew together as shown. Press seams open to reduce bulk.

QUILT ASSEMBLY

1. Lay out (6) tulip blocks and 1 background 2" x 43-1/2" strip as shown. Sew together to make quilt top. Press seams open to reduce bulk.

2. Sew a 2" x 43-1/2" background strip to bottom and top of quilt top. Press seams open to reduce bulk.

3. Sew a 2" x 38" background strip to each side of the quilt top. Press seams open to reduce bulk.

FINISHING THE QUILT

1. Layer the quilt top, batting and backing together. Quilt as desired.

2. Cut 2-1/2" strips from binding fabric and sew together, end to end, to make one long binding strip. Press seams open.

3. Press strip wrong sides together. Sew to front of quilt along raw edges. Fold binding to the back, covering raw edges, and hand stitch in place.

Color is a power which directly influences the soul.

—Wassily Kandinsky

Color Love

Finished size: 42" x 42"

MATERIALS

(24) 10" squares assorted color wheel spectrum prints
(10) fat quarters assorted low volume grays/whites
1-½ yards backing fabric
½ yard binding fabric
QCR Mini Ruler (QCRM)

GENERAL CUTTING INSTRUCTIONS

From (16) of (24) 10" color spectrum prints, cut:

(1) 4-½" x 7-½" for a total of 16 pieces

From 8 of the leftover pieces, cut:

(1) 4" square for a total of 8 squares

From the remaining (8) 10" unused squares, cut:

(1) 4" square for a total of 8 squares

From *each* low volume fat quarter, follow the diagram to cut:

(3) 4" for a total of 30 squares. Set 2 aside.
(7) 5" for a total of 70 squares. Set 2 aside.
(2) 5-½" for a total of 20 squares.
   Set 4 aside. Cut the 16 squares in half diagonally to make 32 triangles.

5" x 5"	5½" x 5½"	5½" x 5½"
5" x 5"	5" x 5"	5" x 5"
5" x 5"	5" x 5"	5" x 5"
	4" x 4"	4" x 4"	4" x 4"

WOF = width of fabric
Read through Using the QCR Mini Ruler,
pages 6-10 before beginning this project.

CUTTING WITH THE QCR MINI RULER

1. From the 5" low volume squares, stack a few, and align the adjoining sides along the dashed "V" lines on the QCRM ruler. Cut in the curved cutout to make A and B shapes. Repeat for all 5" low volume squares to make (68) A and (68) B shapes.

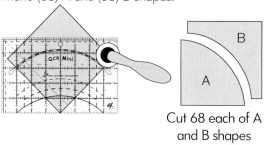

Cut 68 each of A
and B shapes

2. From the 4-½" x 7-½" color spectrum prints, stack a few, and align the adjoining sides along the dashed "V" lines on the QCRM ruler. Cut in the curved cutout to make A shapes. Repeat on the opposite diagonal corner as shown. Continue cutting all pieces to make a total of (32) color spectrum print A shapes. Discard pieces of fabric.

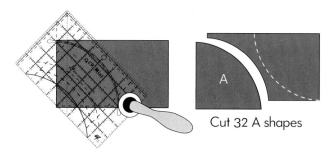

Cut 32 A shapes

3. From the 5-½" low volume triangles, stack a few, and measure in ½" on each diagonal point and trim as shown.

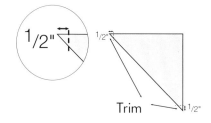

Trim

4. Position the QCRM ruler so the curved cutout lays over the points as shown. Cut in the curved cutout to make (32) low volume B pieces. Discard small pieces of fabric.

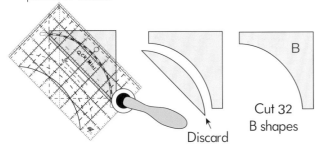

Cut 32
B shapes

Discard

PIECING THE CURVES

1. Lay out the following, mixing up low volume stacks to ensure variety when piecing low volume to low volume shapes.

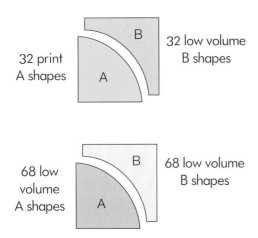

32 print
A shapes

32 low volume
B shapes

68 low
volume
A shapes

68 low volume
B shapes

2. Referring to the diagram, position a low volume A shape on a low volume B shape, right sides together, with B extending 1/2" beyond A.

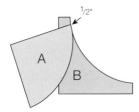

1/2"

3. Hold one shape in each hand and slowly bring the curved edges together while stitching a 1/4" seam. Press seam toward A and press front and back of AB unit.

4. Repeat for all A and B low volume shapes and print/low volume shapes to make (68) AB low volume units and (32) AB print/low volume units.

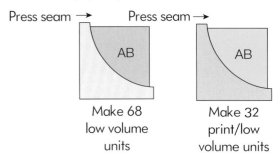

Press seam →   Press seam →

Make 68
low volume
units

Make 32
print/low
volume units

SQUARING UP THE AB UNITS

Square up the AB units to 4" squares. Position the QCRM on AB as shown, with the B piece at the top right position. Leave an 1/8" from curved seam to outer edges. Trim right side and top. Lift ruler, rotate block, reposition QCRM, aligning previously trimmed edges with the 4" marks on the ruler. Trim right side and top. Repeat for all AB units.

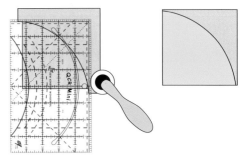

QUILT ASSEMBLY

1. Referring to the Quilt Top Assembly, lay out AB units and 4" squares as shown.

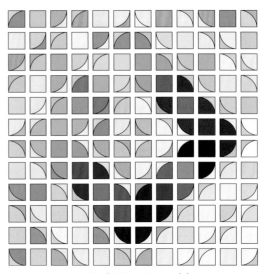

Quilt Top Assembly

2. Sew the units together in rows. Press seams open. Sew the rows together to make quilt top.

FINISHING THE QUILT

1. Layer the quilt top, batting and backing together. Quilt as desired.

2. Cut 2-1/2" strips from binding fabric and sew together, end to end, to make one long binding strip. Press seams open.

3. Press strip wrong sides together. Sew to front of quilt along raw edges. Fold binding to the back, covering raw edges, and hand stitch in place.

'For where thou art,
there is the
world itself,
And where thou art
not, desolation'
—William Shakespeare
Henry IV, Part 2

Heart Beat

Finished size: 20" x 66"

(8) ¼ yard assorted red fabric cuts
(do not use fat quarters)
1-¼ yards background fabric
2 yards backing fabric
½ yard binding fabric
QCR Mini Ruler (QCRM)

From (1) ¼ yard red fabric, cut:
(8) 1" x WOF strips

From remaining ¼ yard red fabric cuts, cut:
(6) 1-½" x WOF for a total of 42 strips. Set 2 strips aside to use for another project.

From background fabric, cut:
(2) 5-½" x WOF strips. From the strips, cut
(12) 5-½" squares. Cut in half diagonally
for 24 triangles.
(1) 4-½" x WOF strip. From strip, cut:
(4) 4-½" x 7-½" pieces
(1) 4" x WOF strip. From strip, cut:
(8) 4" squares
(2) 2" x WOF strips. From strips, cut:
(3) 2" x 14-½" sashing strips
(5) 3-½" x WOF strips.
Sew strips together end to end and cut:
(2) 3-½" x 61" border strips
(2) 3-½" x 20" border strips

WOF = width of fabric
Read through Using the QCR Mini Ruler,
pages 6-10 before beginning this project.

1. Select a mix of (3) 1-½" x WOF and (2) 1" x WOF assorted red strips. Randomly lay out the (5) strips and sew together as shown. Press seams in same direction. Repeat to make (2) 4-½" x WOF strip sets.

2. Cut (8) 4-½" squares from each strip set for a total of (16) squares.

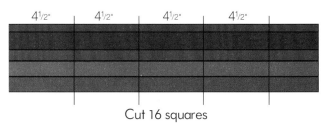

Cut 16 squares

3. Select a mix of (4) 1-½" x WOF and (1) 1" x WOF assorted red strips. Randomly lay out the 5 strips and sew together as shown. Press seams in same direction. From strip set cut (8) 5" squares.

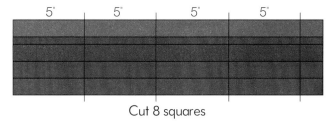

Cut 8 squares

4. Select a mix of (3) 1-½" x WOF and (1) 1" x WOF assorted red strips. Randomly lay out the 4 strips and sew together as shown. Press seams in same direction. Repeat to make (3) 4" x WOF strip sets. Cut 4" squares from the strip sets for a total of (24) squares.

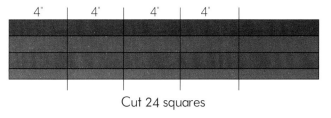

Cut 24 squares

CUTTING WITH THE QCR MINI RULER

1. Position the QCRM on a 4-1/2" square with the stripped piecing horizontal. Place the curved cutout over opposite diagonal corners as shown, and cut in the curved cut to make an A shape. Discard small pieces of fabric. Repeat to make 16 horizontal A shapes.

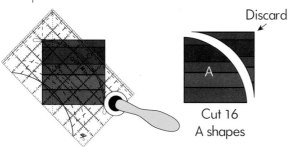

Discard

Cut 16
A shapes

2. Position the QCRM on a 5" square with the stripped piecing vertical. Align the sides along the dashed "V" lines on the QCRM ruler. Cut in the curved cutout to make A and B shapes. Make a total of (8) A and B shapes.

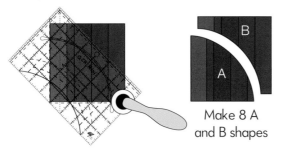

Make 8 A
and B shapes

3. From the 5-1/2" background triangles, stack a few, and measure in 1/2" on each diagonal point and trim as shown. Position the QCRM ruler so the curved cutout lays over the points as shown. Cut in curved cutout to make B shapes. Discard small pieces of fabric. Repeat to make (24) B background shapes.

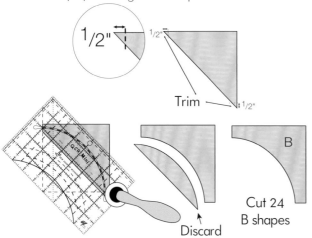

1/2"

Trim

Cut 24
B shapes

Discard

4. From the (4) 4-1/2" x 7-1/2" background pieces, stack a few, and align the adjoining sides along the dashed "V" lines on the QCRM ruler as shown. Cut in the curved cutout to make A shapes. Repeat on the opposite diagonal corner and align the adjoining sides along dashed "V" lines on the QCRM ruler as shown. Cut in the curved cutout to make A shapes. Repeat to make (8) A shapes. Discard small pieces of fabric.

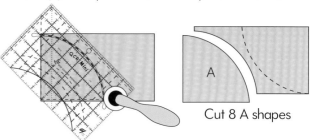

Cut 8 A shapes

PIECING THE CURVES

1. Sew the following sets together:

16 A red strip shapes
16 B background shapes

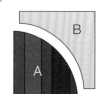

8 A red strip shapes
8 B background shapes

8 A background shapes
8 B red strip shapes

2. Referring to the diagram, position an A shape on a B shape, right sides together, with B extending 1/2" beyond A.

1/2"

3. Hold one shape in each hand and slowly bring the curved edges together while stitching a 1/4" seam. Press seam toward A and press front and back of AB unit. Repeat for all A and B shapes to make (32) AB units.

Press seam

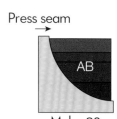

Make 32
AB units

SQUARING UP THE AB SHAPES

Square up the AB units to 4" squares. Position the QCRM on AB as shown, with the B piece at the top right position. Leave an 1/8" from curved seam to outer edges. Trim right and top. Lift ruler, rotate block, reposition QCRM, aligning previously trimmed edges with the 4" marks on the ruler. Trim side and top. Repeat for all AB units.

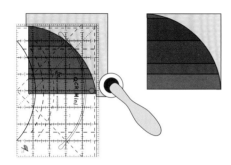

BLOCK ASSEMBLY

1. Lay out AB units and 4" blocks as shown.

2. Sew the units together in rows. Press seams open. Sew the rows together to make blocks. Press seams open. Repeat to make (4) 14-1/2" square woven heart blocks.

QUILT ASSEMBLY

1. Following Quilt Assembly Diagram, lay out heart blocks and sashing as shown. Sew sashing between heart blocks. Press seams towards sashing to complete quilt center.

2. Lay out quilt center and borders. Sew side borders to quilt center. Press seams away from center. Sew top and bottom border to quilt and press seams away from center.

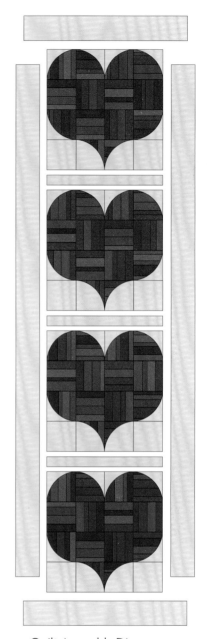

Quilt Assembly Diagram

FINISHING THE QUILT

1. Layer the quilt top, batting and backing together. Quilt as desired.

2. Cut 2-1/2" strips from binding fabric and sew together, end to end, to make one long binding strip. Press seams open.

3. Press strip wrong sides together. Sew to front of quilt along raw edges. Fold binding to the back, covering raw edges, and hand stitch in place.

'*Hope*'
is the thing
with feathers—
That perches
in the soul—
And *sings*
the tune without
the words—
And never stops,
—at all—

—Emily Dickinson

Bird Song

Finished size: 32" x 63"

MATERIALS

(6) assorted green print fat quarters for leaves
(2) 5" blue squares for Bird 1
(2) 5" blue squares for Bird 2
(2) 5" blue squares for Bird 3
(1) 5" gold square for beaks
⅛ yard fabric for stems
2-¼ yards background fabric
½ yard binding fabric
QCR Mini Ruler (QCRM)

GENERAL CUTTING INSTRUCTIONS

 From *each* of 3 green fat quarters, cut:
(5) 4-½" x 7-½" pieces

 From *each* of 3 green fat quarters, cut:
(4) 4-½" x 7-½" pieces

 From gold beak fabric, cut:
(3) 1-½" squares

 From stem fabric, cut:
(4) ¾" x WOF strips.
   Sew strips together end to end and cut:
   (1) ¾" x 63-½"
   (1) ¾" x 28-½"
   (1) ¾" x 25"
   (1) ¾" x 7-½"
   (1) ¾" x 4"

From background fabric, cut:
(5) 5-½" x WOF strips. From strips, cut:
   (32) 5-½" squares
   Cut squares in half, diagonally, and
   discard one triangle.
(4) 7-½" x WOF strips. From strips, cut:
   (36) 4" x 7-½" pieces
   (2) 4-½" x 7-½" piece
(1) 11" x WOF strip. From strip cut:
   (1) 11" square
   (2) 4" x 11" pieces
(2) 4" x WOF strip. From strip, cut:
   (1) 4" x 25" strip
   (5) 4" squares
(2) 1-½" x WOF strips. Sew strips end to end
   and cut:
   (1) 1-½" x 63-½" strip

WOF = width of fabric
Read through Using the QCR Mini Ruler,
pages 6-10 before beginning this project.

CUTTING WITH THE QCR MINI RULER

1. From the (6) 5" blue bird squares, stack a few and align the adjoining sides along the dashed "V" lines on the QCRM ruler. Cut in the curved cutout (red dashed line) to make a total of (6) A and B shapes.

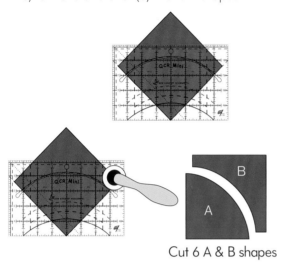

Cut 6 A & B shapes

2. From the 4-1/2" x 7-1/2" assorted green prints and 2 background pieces of the same size, stack a few, and align the adjoining sides along the dashed "V" lines on the QCRM ruler. Cut in the curved cutout to make A shapes. Repeat on the opposite diagonal corner. Repeat using all assorted green prints for a total of (54) assorted green A shapes and (2) background A shapes. Discard small pieces of fabric.

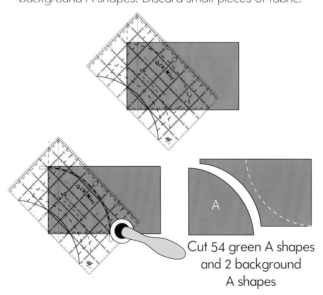

Cut 54 green A shapes
and 2 background
A shapes

3. From the background fabric triangles, stack a few, measure and mark 1/2" on both points and trim as shown. Position the QCRM on the triangle with the curved cutout on the 1/2" marks. Cut in the curved cutout to make B shapes. Repeat with all triangles to make a total of (63) B shapes. Discard small pieces of fabric.

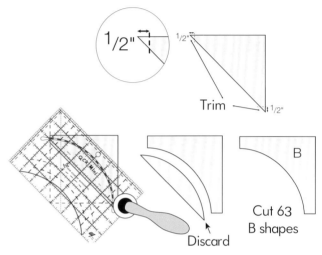

Cut 63
B shapes

Discard

PIECING THE CURVES

1. Using (54) assorted green A shapes and (54) background B shapes, position an assorted green A shape on a background B shape, right sides together, with B extending 1/2" beyond A.

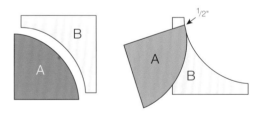

2. Hold one shape in each hand and slowly bring the curved edges together while stitching a 1/4" seam. Press seam toward A and press front and back of AB unit. Repeat with all assorted green shapes and background shapes for a total of (54) assorted green/background AB units.

Press seam →

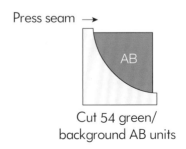

Cut 54 green/
background AB units

PIECING THE CURVES OF THE BIRDS

1. Lay out the following A and B pieces to make bird bodies and tails:

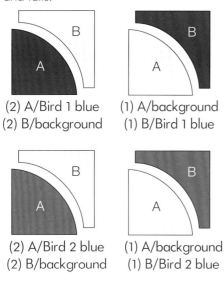

(2) A/Bird 1 blue   (1) A/background
(2) B/background   (1) B/Bird 1 blue

(2) A/Bird 2 blue   (1) A/background
(2) B/background   (1) B/Bird 2 blue

(2) A/Bird 3 blue   (1) A/background
(2) B/background   (1) B/Bird 3 blue

2. To sew the sets together, position an A shape on a B shape, right sides together, with B extending ½" beyond A. Hold one shape in each hand and slowly bring the curved edges together while stitching a ¼" seam. Press seam toward A and press front and back of AB unit. Repeat with all A and B shapes to make (6) blue/background AB units for bodies and (3) background/blue AB units for tails.

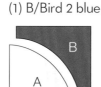

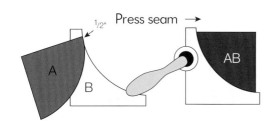

3. For each 1-½" gold square, fold corner to corner, wrong sides together and finger press. Fold again and press to make quarter square shapes for bird beaks.

 Make 3

MAKING BIRD HEADS

1. Lay out (3) bird blue AB units for bird heads as shown. (This will create (2) bird heads facing to the right and (1) facing left.)

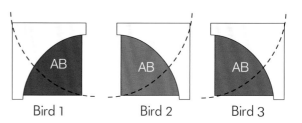

2. Position the QCRM on each AB unit with curve cutout over diagonal points and cut in curve cutout. Discard small pieces of fabric.

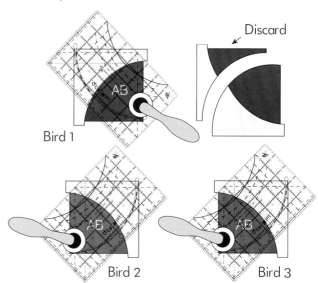

3. Position a gold bird beak on each of the AB bird head units as shown in diagram. Pin in place.

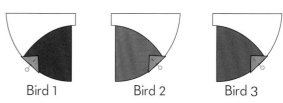

4. Using an AB bird head unit, position the unit on a B background shape, right sides together, but with B extending only ¼" beyond AB unit. Hold one shape in each hand and slowly bring the curved edges together while stitching a ¼" seam. Press seam toward AB and

press front and back of ABB unit. Repeat to make (3) ABB bird head units.

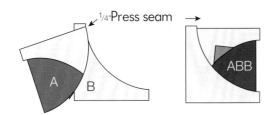

5. Lay out 2 AB bird tail shapes as shown for Birds 1 and 2. Position the QCRM on each AB unit with curve cutout over diagonal points and cut in curve cutout. Discard small pieces of fabric.

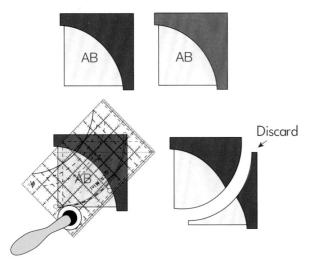

6. From 2 AB bird tails, position the AB unit on a matching B blue shape, right sides together, but with B extending **only** 1/4" beyond the AB unit. Hold one shape in each hand and slowly bring the curved edges together while stitching a 1/4" seam. Press seam toward AB and press front and back of ABB unit. Repeat to make (2) ABB bird tail units.

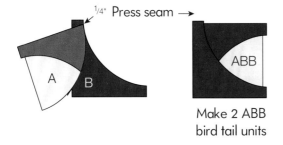

Make 2 ABB bird tail units

SQUARING UP THE AB UNITS

Square up the AB and ABB units to 4" squares. Position the QCRM on AB as shown, with the B piece at the top right position. Leave an 1/8" from curved seam to outer edges. Trim right and top. Lift ruler, rotate block, reposition QCRM, aligning previously trimmed edges with the 4" marks on the ruler. Trim side and top. Repeat for all AB and ABB units.

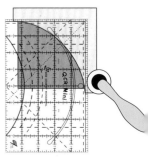

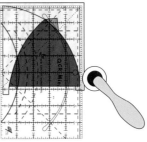

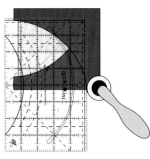

BIRD ASSEMBLY

Lay out bird AB, ABB bird head, ABB tail, and (1) background 4" square. Sew the units together to form rows. Press seams open. Sew rows together to complete block. Press seams open.

Bird 1

Bird 2

Bird 3

LEAF ASSEMBLY

Pair up and lay out matching AB leaf units as shown. Sew pairs together to make (28) leaf units. Press seams open. Make 11 left leaf units and 16 right leaf units.

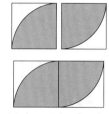

Make 11 leaf units   Make 16 leaf units

QUILT AND STEM ASSEMBLY

Referring to Quilt Assembly Section Diagram, on page 32, lay out sections as shown.

Section 1

(6) leaf sections and (12) 4" x 7-1/2" background pieces. Sew sections and pieces together in a vertical row. Press seams open. Trim 1/4" off the right side of the Section 1. Sew a 3/4" x 63-1/2" stem section to the right side to complete Section 1. Press seams towards stem.

Section 2

(8) leaf sections and (10) 4" x 7-1/2" background pieces. Press seam toward stem. Sew sections and pieces together and press seams open. Sew a 1-1/2" x 63-1/2" background strip to the right side of Section 2. Press seams toward stem.

Section 3

(3) leaf sections and (4) 4" x 7-1/2" background pieces. Sew sections and pieces together and press seams open. Trim 1/4" off right side of Section 3. Sew 3/4" x 25" stem to right side. Press seam toward stem.

Section 4

(4) leaf sections

(1) 4" x 25" background piece

(2) 4" background squares and (1) 3/4" x 4" stem. Trim 1/4" off right side of first 4" piece. Sew pieces together and press seams toward stem.

(2) 4" x 7-1/2" pieces and (1) 3/4" x 7-1/2" stem piece. Trim 1/4" off right long side of first piece. Sew pieces together and press seams toward stem.

Referring to Quilt Assembly Section Diagram, lay out sections as shown. Sew pieces together to make Section 4. Press seams open.

Sew Sections 3 and 4 together. Press seams toward stem.

Section 5

(2) 4" x 11" pieces
(3) 4" x 7-1/2" pieces
(2) leaf sections
Bird blocks 2 and 3 (beaks will point the same way)
Sew sections together. Trim 1/4" off right side of Section 5 and sew a 3/4" x 28-1/2" stem to right side. Press seam towards stem.

Section 6

(4) leaf sections and (4) 4" x 7-1/2" background pieces. Sew together to make Section 6 and press seams open.

Lay out sections 5 and 6 and sew together. Press seams towards stem.

Section 7

Bird 1, (1) 11" background square, and
(1) 4" x 7-1/2" background piece to make Section 7.
Sew pieces together and press seams open.

QUILT ASSEMBLY

1. Referring to Quilt Assembly Diagram below, layout sections as shown.

2. To finish the quilt assembly, sew Sections 3/4, 5/6 and 7 together in a vertical row. Sew the two remaining vertical rows together to complete the quilt top.

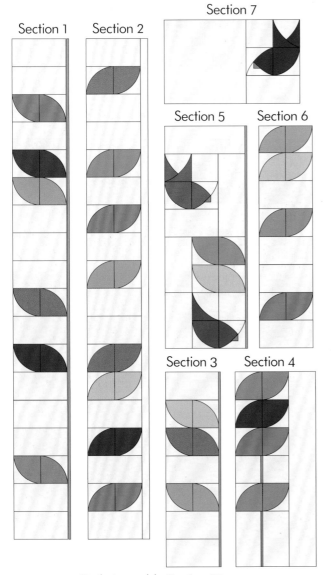

Quilt Assembly Section Diagram

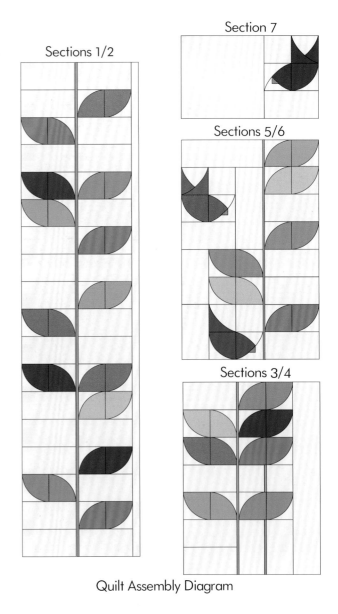

Quilt Assembly Diagram

FINISHING THE QUILT

1. Layer the quilt top, batting and backing together. Quilt as desired.

2. Cut 2-½" strips from binding fabric and sew together, end to end, to make one long binding strip. Press seams open.

3. Press strip wrong sides together. Sew to front of quilt along raw edges. Fold binding to the back, covering raw edges, and hand stitch in place.

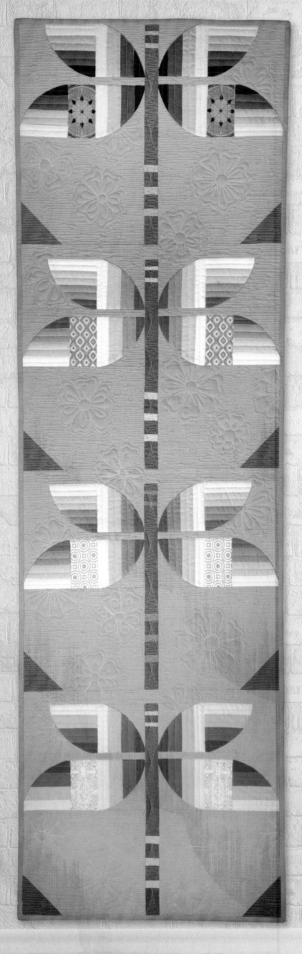

Always maintain a
kind of summer
Even in the middle of winter

—Henry David Thoreau

Spring Wings

Finished size: 19" x 63"

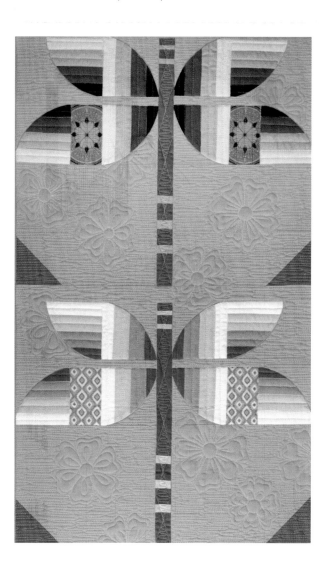

MATERIALS

(16) 2-1/2" WOF strips
  (4 blues, 4 purples, 4 reds, 4 grays)
(4) 5" print squares to coordinate with the
  4 colors above, for accent in wings
(4) 2" x 5" coordinating solids for
  accent bands in bodies
1/3 yard dark gray for bodies
1 fat quarter for accent setting triangles
1-1/2 yards background fabric
1-3/4 yards backing fabric
1/2 yard binding fabric
QCR Mini Ruler (QCRM)

GENERAL CUTTING INSTRUCTIONS

 From *each* of the (16) 2-1/2" WOF strips, cut:
(1) 1-1/2" by WOF strips for wings

 From *each* 5" print accent square, cut:
(2) 2-1/2 x 4" pieces for a total of 8 wing accents

 From *each* solid accent body band pieces, cut:
(2) 3/4" x 1-1/2" pieces
(3) 1" x 1-1/2" pieces

 From dark gray, cut:
(2) 1-1/2" x WOF strips. From the strips, cut:
  (8) 1" x 1-1/2" pieces
  (8) 1-1/2" squares
  (4) 1-1/2" x 2-1/2" pieces
  (4) 1-1/2" x 8-1/2" pieces

 From the fat quarter, cut:
(8) 3-1/2" x 3-1/2" squares for
  accent setting triangles

 From background fabric, cut:
(3) 5-1/2" by WOF strips. From the strips, cut:
  (16) 5-1/2" squares. Cut squares in half,
  diagonally, for a total of 32 triangles
(1) 4" x WOF strip. From the strip, cut:
  (8) 2-1/2" x 4" pieces
(2) 1-1/2" x WOF strips. From the strips, cut:
  (3) 1-1/2" x 19-1/2" sashing pieces
(2) 1" x WOF strips. From the strips, cut:
  (8) 1" x 9-1/2" strips
(2) 8" x WOF strips. From the strips, cut:
  (8) 8" x 9-1/2" pieces

WOF = width of fabric
Read through Using the QCR Mini Ruler,
pages 6-10 before beginning this project.

STRIP PIECING THE WING SETS

1. Lay out each set by color, from lightest to darkest as shown. Sew together along long sides and press seams in same direction. Repeat for each colorway to make a total (4) strip sets.

2. Cut EACH color set into (8) 4-1/2" pieced squares for a total of 32 squares.

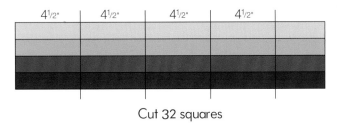

Cut 32 squares

CUTTING WITH THE QCR MINI RULER

1. Lay out (4) 4-1/2" pieced squares of the same colorway with the lightest fabrics on the sides as shown.

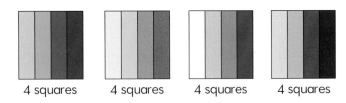

| 4 squares | 4 squares | 4 squares | 4 squares |

2. Position the QCRM on a block, aligning two adjoining sides along the dashed "V" lines as shown. (Use the diagram below to ensure the QCRM ruler is placed correctly on the block.) Using a rotary cutter, cut in the curved cutout to make an A shape. Discard small pieces of fabric. Repeat for all 4-1/2" pieced squares to make (8) A shapes.

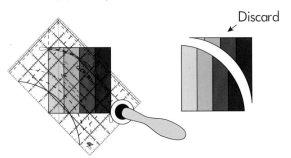

Discard

3. Lay out (4) 4-1/2" pieced squares of the same colorway with the lightest fabrics on the bottom as shown.

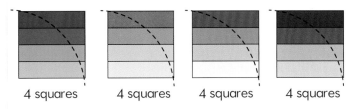

| 4 squares | 4 squares | 4 squares | 4 squares |

4. Position the QCRM on a block, aligning two adjoining sides along the dashed "V" lines as shown. (Use the diagram below to ensure the QCRM ruler is placed correctly on the block.) Using a rotary cutter, cut in the curved cutout to make an A shape. Discard small pieces of fabric. Repeat for all 4-1/2" pieced squares to make (8) A shapes.

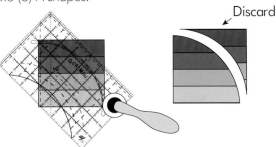

Discard

5. Stack a few 5-1/2" background triangles. Measure in 1/2" on both points and trim.

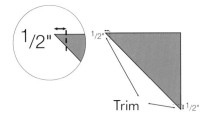

1/2"   1/2"

Trim   1/2"

6. Position QCRM so the curved cutout lays over points as shown. Using a rotary cutter, cut in the ruler's curved cutout to make B shapes. Discard small pieces of fabric. Repeat to make (32) B background shapes.

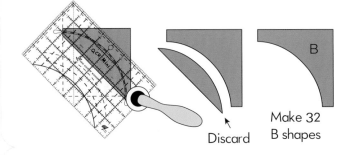

B

Discard   Make 32 B shapes

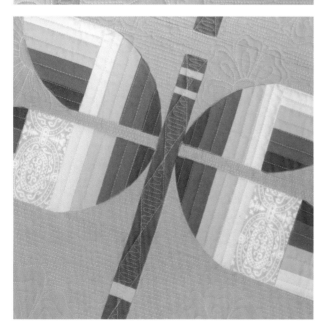

PIECING THE CURVES

1. Lay out the color A shapes and background B shapes as shown.

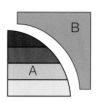

2. Position an A shape on a B shape, right sides together, with 1/2" of B extending beyond A.

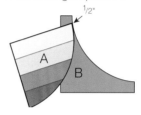

3. Hold one shape in each hand and slowly bring the curved edges together while stitching a ¼" seam. Press seam toward A and press front and back of AB unit. Repeat for all A and B shapes to make (32) AB units.

Press seam →

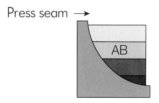

Make 32 AB units

SQUARING UP THE AB UNITS

Square up the AB units to 4" squares. Position the QCRM on AB as shown, with the B piece at the top right position. Leave an ⅛" from curved seam to outer edge. Trim right and top. Lift ruler, rotate block, reposition QCRM, aligning previously trimmed edges with the 4" marks on the ruler. Trim side and top. Repeat for all AB units.

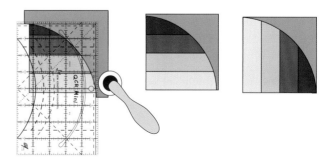

DRAGONFLY BODY ASSEMBLY

Lay out body pieces and coordinating color focus pieces as shown. Working from left to right sew the pieces together. Press seams towards color bands. Repeat to make (4) body pieces measuring 1-1/2" x 15-1/2".

DRAGONFLY BLOCK ASSEMBLY

1. Following the diagram below and working with one color at a time, lay out AB wing units, 1 pieced body, (2) 2-1/2" x 4" wing accent pieces, (2) 1" x 9-1/2" background pieces, (2) 2-1/2" x 4" background pieces, (2) 8" x 9-1/2" background pieces.

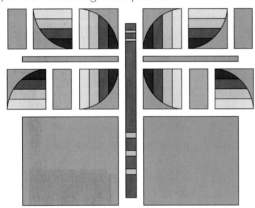

2. Working with one side of the dragonfly at a time, sew units together to form rows. Sew rows and background pieces together in order shown. Press seams open and repeat for the other side. Sew each side to the dragonfly body. Repeat to make 4 dragonfly blocks. Blocks should measure 15-1/2" x 19-1/2".

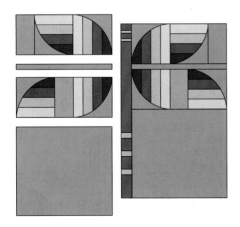

ADDING ACCENT TRIANGLE PIECES (OPTIONAL)

1. Draw a diagonal line on the wrong side of all 3-1/2" square accent pieces.

2. Position 1 on each lower corner of dragonfly blocks aligning edges, as shown. Sew on drawn line. Trim fabric 1/4" from sewn line. Press open. Repeat on all dragonfly blocks.

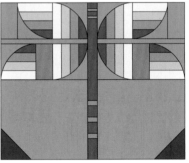

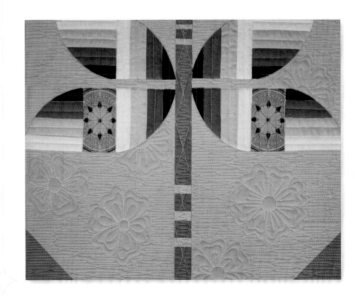

DRAGONFLY RUNNER ASSEMBLY

1. Lay out the 4 dragonfly blocks as shown, with 1-1/2" x 19-1/2" sashing strips between blocks. Sew sashing to blocks and press seams.

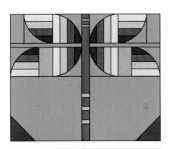

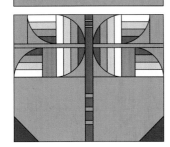

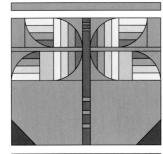

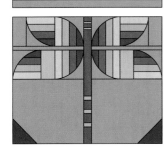

2. Layer the quilt top, batting and backing together. Quilt as desired.

3. Cut 2-1/2" strips from binding fabric and sew together, end to end, to make one long binding strip. Press seams open.

4. Press strip wrong sides together. Sew to front of quilt along raw edges. Fold binding to the back, covering raw edges, and hand stitch in place.

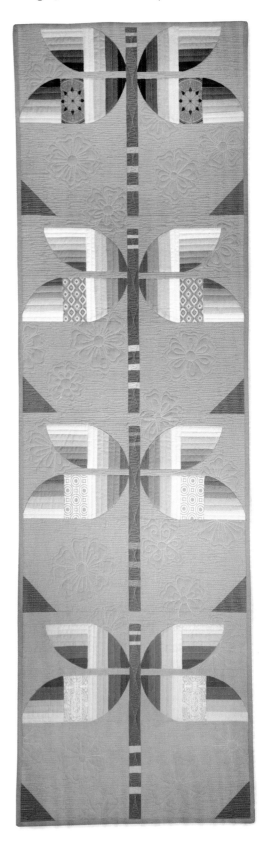

"Hold me gently in your hand, Lift me to the sunlight, I will shine for you,
Be *your sea treasure* and Never seek another."

—Richard Morgan

Sea Glass

Finished size: 28" x 35"

MATERIALS

(10) Fat Quarters of assorted prints
½ yard solid tan fabric
1-¼ yard backing fabric
½ yard binding fabric
QCR Mini Ruler (QCRM)

GENERAL CUTTING INSTRUCTIONS

 From 9 assorted fat quarters, cut:
(6) 5" squares

 From 1 assorted fat quarter, cut:
(8) 5" squares

 From solid tan fabric, cut:
(3) 5" x WOF strips. From strips, cut:
    (18) 5" squares

WOF = width of fabric
Read through Using the QCR Mini Ruler, pages 6-10 before beginning this project.

CUTTING WITH THE QCR MINI RULER

1. From the 5" assorted fabric and solid fabric squares, stack a few and align the adjoining sides along the dashed "V" lines on the QCRM ruler. Cut in the curved cutout (red dashed line).

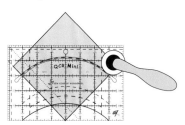

2. Repeat for all 5" squares to make a total of (62) assorted A and B shapes and (18) solid A and B shapes.

Cut 62 assorted print A and B shapes

Cut 18 solid A and B shapes

PIECING THE CURVES

NOTE: This is a "design wall" quilt. Lay out the A and B shapes on your wall as shown in the diagram.

1. Working with one A and B set at a time, position the A shape on the B shape, right sides together with B extending ½" beyond A shape.

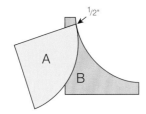

2. Hold one shape in each hand and slowly bring the curved edges together while stitching a ¼" seam. Press seam toward A and press front and back of AB unit. Lay each sewn set back on the design wall after sewing to ensure placement stays consistent with design. Repeat with all A and B sets to make a total of 80 AB units.

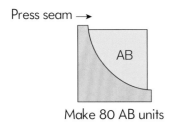

Make 80 AB units

SQUARING UP THE AB SHAPES

1. Square up the AB units to 4" squares. Position the QCRM on AB as shown, with the B piece at the top right position. Leave an ⅛" from curved seam to outer edges. Trim right and top. Lift ruler, rotate block, reposition QCRM, aligning previously trimmed edges with the 4" marks on the ruler. Trim side and top. Repeat for all AB units.

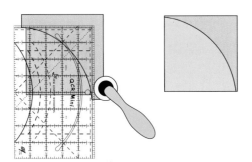

2. Reposition AB units back on the design wall for consistent design.

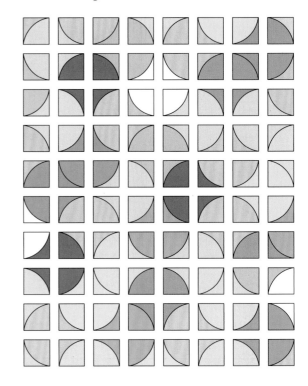

QUILT ASSEMBLY

1. Working with the first row on your design wall, sew AB units together in order. Press seams open.

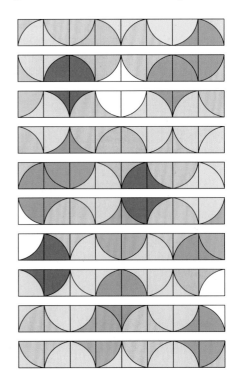

2. Repeat to sew all rows together, and sew rows together to finish quilt top. Press seams open.

FINISHING THE QUILT

1. Layer the quilt top, batting and backing together. Quilt as desired.

2. Cut 2-½" strips from binding fabric and sew together, end to end, to make one long binding strip. Press seams open.

3. Press strip wrong sides together. Sew to front of quilt along raw edges. Fold binding to the back, covering raw edges, and hand stitch in place.

What if you finally saw that the *sunflowers,* turning toward the sun all day and every day—who knows how, but they do it—were more precious, more meaningful than *gold.*

—Mary Oliver

Soak Up The Sun

Finished size: 56" x 56"

MATERIALS

(8) Fat Quarters of assorted yellow prints
   for flowers
(4) 10" squares of assorted green prints
   for leaves
(4) Fat Quarters of assorted gray prints
   for flower centers
(1) yard *each* of background fabric in light blue,
   light gray, medium gray, and white
4 yards backing fabric
½ yard binding fabric
QCR Mini Ruler (QCRM)

GENERAL CUTTING INSTRUCTIONS

 From *each* assorted yellow fat quarter, cut:
(9) 5" squares for a total of 72

 From *each* assorted green 10" square, cut:
(4) 5" squares for a total of 16

 From *each* assorted gray fabric fat quarter cut:
(5) 4-½" x 7-½" pieces for a total 20.
   Set 2 aside.

 From *each* background fabric, cut:
(2) 4-½" x 7-½" pieces for a total of 8
(2) 5-1/2" by WOF strips. From the strips, cut:
(11) 5-½" squares. Cut the 5-½" squares
   in half diagonally for a total of
   (88) 5-1/2" triangles.

(3) 4" x WOF strips. From strips, cut:
   (29) 4" squares for a total of (116) 4" squares

WOF = width of fabric
Read through Using the QCR Mini Ruler,
pages 6-10 before beginning this project.

CUTTING WITH THE QCR MINI RULER

1. From the (16) 5" assorted green squares, stack a few and align the adjoining sides along the dashed "V" lines on the QCRM ruler. Cut in the curved cutout (red dashed line) to make a total of (16) A and B shapes. Repeat for the (72) assorted yellow 5" squares for a total of (72) A and B shapes. Set aside (36) assorted yellow B shapes; they will not be used in this project.

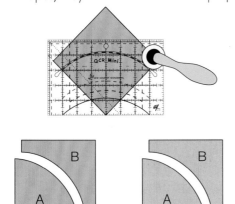

Cut 16 assorted green   Cut 72 assorted yellow
A and B shapes   A and B shapes

2. From the (18) 4-1/2" x 7-1/2" assorted gray prints, stack a few, and align the adjoining sides along the dashed "V" lines on the QCRM ruler. Cut in the curved cutout to make A shapes. Repeat on the opposite diagonal corner as shown, for a total of (36) assorted A shapes. Repeat for the (8) assorted background 4-1/2" x 7-1/2" pieces for a total of (16) A shapes. Discard small pieces of fabric.

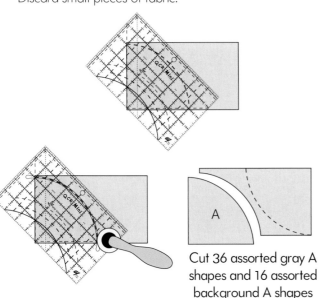

Cut 36 assorted gray A shapes and 16 assorted background A shapes

3. From the background fabric triangles, stack a few, measure and mark 1/2" on both points and trim as shown. Position the QCRM on the triangle with the curved cutout on the 1/2" marks. Cut in the curved cutout to make a total of (88) B shapes.

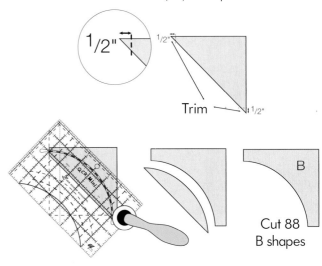

Trim

Cut 88 B shapes

PIECING THE CURVES

1. Layout the following A and B shapes as shown.

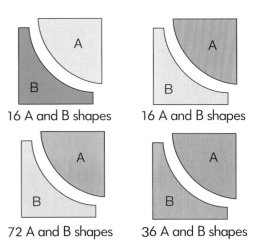

16 A and B shapes   16 A and B shapes

72 A and B shapes   36 A and B shapes

2. Referring to the diagram, position an assorted print A shape on a background B shape, right sides together, with B extending 1/2" beyond A. Hold one shape in each hand and slowly bring the curved edges together while stitching a 1/4" seam. Press seam toward A and press front and back of AB unit.

Press seam →

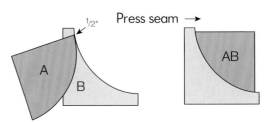

3. Repeat above directions for all A and B shapes to make (16) green/background AB units for leaves, (16) background/green AB units for leaves, (72) assorted yellow/background AB units for flowers, and (36) gray/assorted yellow AB units for flower centers.

 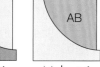

| Make 16 AB leaf units | Make 16 AB leaf units | Make 72 AB flower units | Make 36 AB flower center units |

SQUARING UP THE AB SHAPES

Square up the AB units to 4" squares". Position the QCRM on AB as shown, with the B piece at the top right position. Leave an 1/8" from curved seam to outer edges. Trim right side and top. Lift ruler, rotate block, reposition QCRM, aligning previously trimmed edges with the 4" marks on the ruler. Trim side and top. Repeat for all AB units.

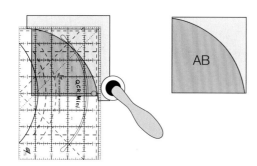

ASSEMBLING THE QUILT TOP

Following the Quilt Top Assembly Diagram, lay out the AB units. Sew units together in rows. Press seams open. Sew rows together to make quilt top. Press seams open.

Quilt Top Assembly Diagram

FINISHING THE QUILT

1. Layer the quilt top, batting and backing together. Quilt as desired.

2. Cut 2-1/2" strips from binding fabric and sew together, end to end, to make one long binding strip. Press seams open.

3. Press strip wrong sides together. Sew to front of quilt along raw edges. Fold binding to the back, covering raw edges, and hand stitch in place.

One *flag,*
One *land,*
One *heart,*
One *hand,*
One nation *evermore!*

—Oliver Wendell Holmes

Freedom's Flag

Finished size: 32" x 38"

MATERIALS

(6) 10" assorted navy squares
1 Fat Quarter—silver/gray focus fabric for stars
3 Fat Quarters—assorted red focus fabrics
1 yard white fabric for stripes
1-¼ yard backing fabric
½ yard binding fabric
QCR Mini Ruler (QCRM)

GENERAL CUTTING INSTRUCTIONS

 From *each* assorted navy focus fabric, cut:
(1) 4-½" x 7-½" pieces for a total of 6
(2) 4" squares for a total of 12

 From silver/gray star fabric, cut:
(6) 5-½" squares. Cut squares in half diagonally
    for a total of (12) 5-½" triangles.
    (3) 4" squares

 From *each* assorted red fabric, cut:
(12) 5" squares for a total of 36

 From white fabric, cut:
(5) 5" x WOF strips. From strips, cut:
    (36) 5" squares

WOF = width of fabric
Read through Using the QCR Mini Ruler,
pages 6-10 before beginning this project.

CUTTING WITH THE QCR MINI RULER

1. From the 5" assorted red fabric and white fabric
    squares, stack a few and align the adjoining sides
    along the dashed "V" lines on the QCRM ruler.
    Cut in the curved cutout (yellow dashed line) to make
    a total of (36) red A and B shapes, and (36) white A
    and B shapes.

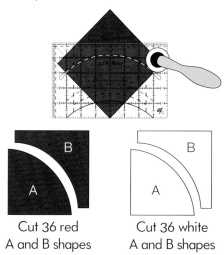

Cut 36 red   Cut 36 white
A and B shapes   A and B shapes

2. From the 4-½" x 7-½" assorted navy fabrics, stack
    a few and align the adjoining sides along the dashed
    "V" lines on the QCRM ruler. Cut in the curved cutout
    to make A shapes. Repeat on the opposite diagonal
    corner as shown. Continue cutting all pieces to make a
    total of (12) navy A shapes. Discard small pieces
    of fabric.

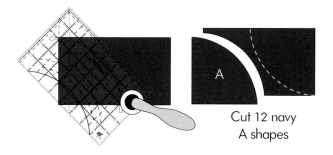

Cut 12 navy
A shapes

3. From the (12) silver/gray triangles, stack a few, measure and mark ½" on both points and trim as shown. Position the QCRM on the triangle with the curved cutout on the ½" marks. Cut in the curved cutout to make a total of (12) B shapes. Discard small fabric pieces.

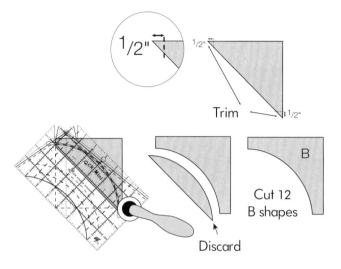

Trim

Cut 12
B shapes

Discard

PIECING THE CURVES

1. Layout A & B shapes as shown.

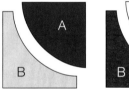

2. Referring to the diagram, position an A shape on a corresponding B shape, right sides together with B extending ½" beyond A. Hold one shape in each hand and slowly bring the curved edges together while stitching a ¼" seam. Press seam toward A and press front and back of AB unit.

Press seam →

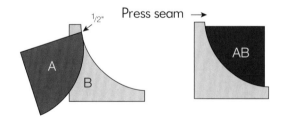

3. Repeat for all A and B shapes to make (12) navy and silver/gray AB units, (36) red/white AB units, and (36) white/red AB units.

Make 12 navy/silver— gray AB units

Make 36 red/white AB units

Make 36 white/red AB units

SQUARING UP THE AB SHAPES

Square up the AB units to 4" squares. Position the QCRM on AB as shown, with the B piece at the top right position. Leave an 1/8" from curved seam to outer edges. Trim right and top. Lift ruler, rotate block, reposition QCRM, aligning previously trimmed edges with the 4" marks on the ruler. Trim side and top. Repeat for all AB units.

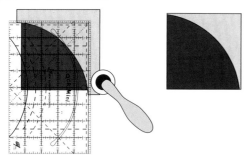

QUILT ASSEMBLY

1. Lay out AB units and squares as shown.

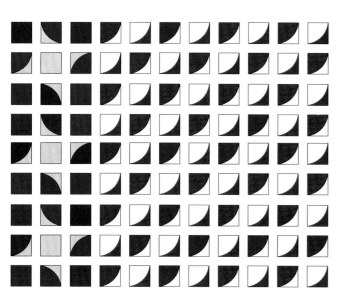

2. Sew units together in rows. Press seams open. Sew rows together to complete the quilt top. Press seams open.

FINISHING THE QUILT

1. Layer the quilt top, batting and backing together. Quilt as desired.

2. Cut 2-1/2" strips from binding fabric and sew together, end to end, to make one long binding strip. Press seams open.

3. Press strip wrong sides together. Sew to front of quilt along raw edges. Fold binding to the back, covering raw edges, and hand stitch in place.

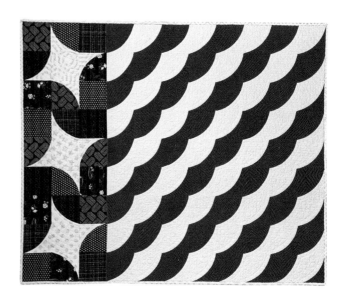

You say *"an hour"* every time. Your hours are much longer than mine.

—David L. Harrison

#arewethereyet

Finished size: 43" x 43"

MATERIALS

(8) assorted color fat quarters for geese
(8) assorted low volume fat quarters for geese
1 yard background fabric
3 yards backing fabric
½ yard binding fabric
QCR Mini Ruler (QCRM)

GENERAL CUTTING INSTRUCTIONS

From *each* assorted color fat quarter, cut:
(8) 5-½" squares for a total of 64.
    (Set aside 6)
    Cut the 58 squares in half diagonally for
    (116) triangles.

From *each* assorted low volume fat quarter, cut:
(8) 4-½" x 7-½" pieces for a total or 64.
    (Set aside 6)

From background fabric, cut:
(3) 10-½" x WOF strips. From strips, cut:
    (3) 7" x 10-½" pieces
    (6) 10-½" x 12-¼" pieces

WOF = width of fabric
Read through Using the QCR Mini Ruler,
pages 6-10 before beginning this project.

CUTTING WITH THE QCR MINI RULER

1. From the (58) 4-½" x 7-½" low volume pieces, stack a few, and align the adjoining sides along the dashed "V" lines on the QCRM ruler. Cut in the curved cutout to make A shapes. Repeat on the opposite diagonal corner as shown, for a total of (116) A shapes. Discard small pieces of fabric.

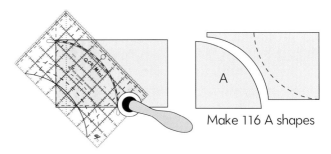

Make 116 A shapes

2. From the assorted color triangles, stack a few and measure and mark ½" on both points. Position the QCRM on the triangle with the curved cutout on the ½" marks. Cut in the curved cutout to make a total of (116) B shapes. Discard small pieces of fabric.

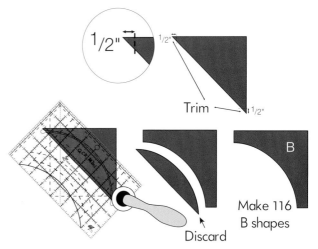

Make 116 B shapes

PIECING THE CURVES

1. Referring to the diagram, position a low volume A shape on a background B shape, right sides together, with B extending ½" beyond A. Hold one shape in each hand and slowly bring the curved edges together

while stitching a ¼" seam. Press seam toward A and press front and back of AB unit.

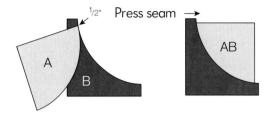

2. Repeat for all A and B shapes for a total of (116) low volume/assorted color AB units.

SQUARING UP THE AB SHAPES

Square up the AB units to 4" squares. Position the QCRM on AB as shown, with the B piece at the top right position. Leave ⅛" from curved seam to outer edges. Trim side and top. Lift ruler, rotate block, reposition QCRM, aligning previously trimmed edges with the 4" marks on the ruler. Trim side and top. Repeat for all AB units.

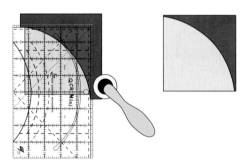

PIECING CURVED FLYING GEESE

Lay out matching AB sets as shown. Sew sets together to make curved geese. Press seam open. Repeat to make (58) 4" x 7-½" curved geese blocks.

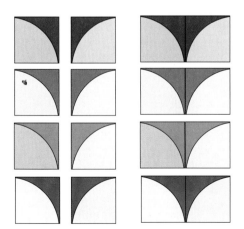

Make 58 curved geese blocks

PIECING THE CURVED GEESE SETS

1. Lay out 4 random geese and measure and mark 1" from corners as shown. Using a straight edge, rotary cut from corners to inch marks and discard small piece.

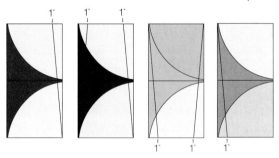

2. Sew geese units in order shown, right sides together, using a scant ¼" seam. Press seams open. Repeat steps 1 and 2 for a total of (6) curved geese blocks.

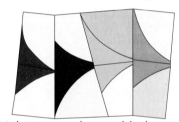

Make 6 curved geese blocks

3. Trim the 4 block sets to 7" x 10-½", trimming the 7" sides first. Trim to 10-½" to finish the (6) block sets.

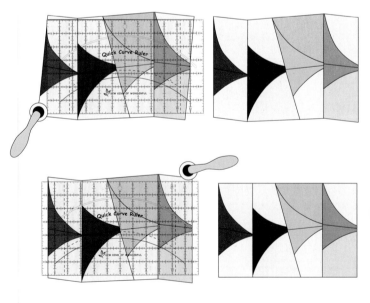

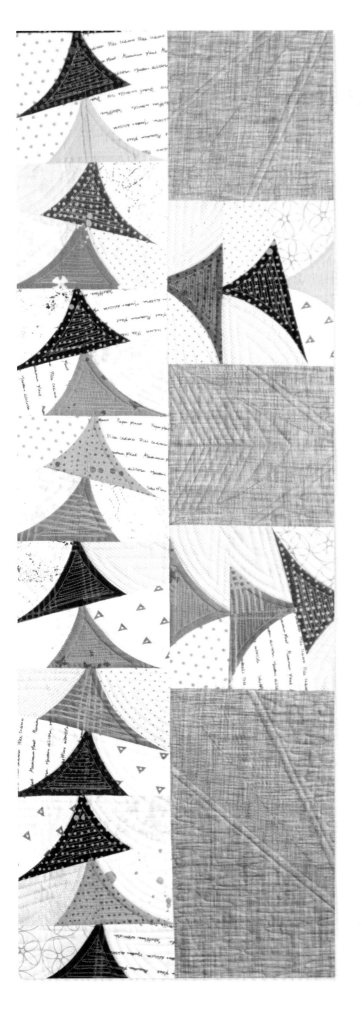

4. Lay out 4 more curved geese sets and measure and mark 1" from corners as shown. Using a straight edge, rotary cut from corners to inch marks and discard small piece. Label (2) as block L and (2) as Block R.

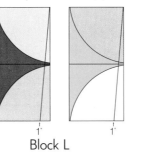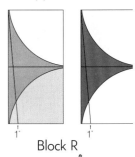

Block L   Block R

5. Divide remaining geese blocks into 2 random color stacks of (16) and (14). Position geese in direction shown.

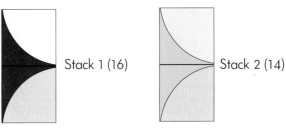

Stack 1 (16)   Stack 2 (14)

6. For the stack of (16), measure and mark 1" along top edge as shown. Using a straight edge, rotary cut from corners to inch marks and discard small piece. Label the stack of (16) as Block S (skinny top).

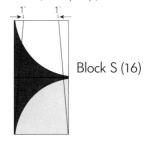

Block S (16)

7. For the stack of (14), measure and mark 1" along bottom edge as shown. Using a straight edge, rotary cut from corners to inch marks and discard small piece. Label the stack of (14) as Block W (wide top).

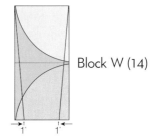

Block W (14)

55

GEESE BLOCK LAYOUT

1. Lay out (1) L, (8) S, (7) W, and (1) R as shown.
   Sew blocks right sides together with a scant ¼" seam.
   Press seams open.

2. Trim the block set to 7" x 43-½", trimming the 7" sides
   first, then trimming the 43-½" long side. Repeat Steps
   1 and 2 to make (2) sets.

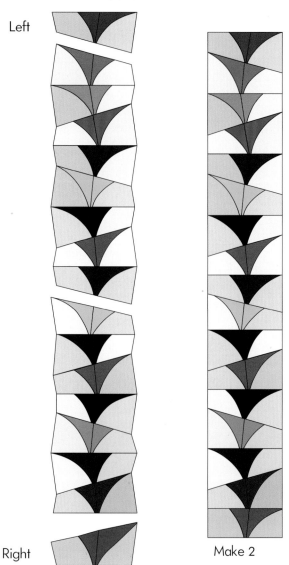

Left

Right

Make 2

LAYOUT AND QUILT ASSEMBLY

1. Referring to the Quilt Assembly Diagram, lay out
   geese sets and background pieces as shown, following
   orientation of geese.

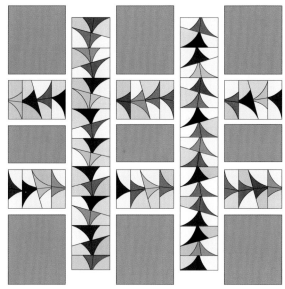

Quilt Assembly Diagram

2. Sew sets and pieces together to form vertical rows.
   Press seams toward background fabric. Sew rows
   together and press seams open to reduce bulk.

FINISHING THE QUILT

1. Layer the quilt top, batting and backing together.
   Quilt as desired.

2. Cut 2-½" strips from binding fabric and sew together,
   end to end, to make one long binding strip. Press
   seams open.

3. Press strip wrong sides together. Sew to front of quilt
   along raw edges. Fold binding to the back, covering
   raw edges, and hand stitch in place.

Bittersweet October.

The mellow, messy, leaf-kicking, perfect pause between the opposing miseries of summer and winter.

—Carol Bishop Hipps

Cider House

Finished size: 35" x 35"

MATERIALS

(8) assorted print fat quarters
(1) green fat quarter
1-¼ yards backing fabric
⅓ yard binding fabric
QCR Mini Ruler (QCRM)

GENERAL CUTTING INSTRUCTIONS

From *each* assorted print fat quarter, cut:
(11) 5" squares for a total of 88 squares

From green fat quarter, cut:
(12) 5" squares

WOF = width of fabric
Read through Using the QCR Mini Ruler,
pages 6-10 before beginning this project.

CUTTING WITH THE QCR MINI RULER

From the 5" assorted print and green squares,
stack a few and align the adjoining sides along the
dashed "V" lines on the QCRM ruler. Cut in the
curved cutout (red dashed line) to make a total of
(100) A and (100) B shapes.

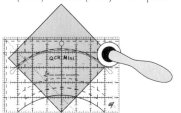

Cut 88 print A and B shapes
12 green A and B shapes

PIECING THE CURVES

NOTE: This is a "design wall" quilt. Lay out the A and
B shapes on your wall to create the apple core and
pinwheel design.

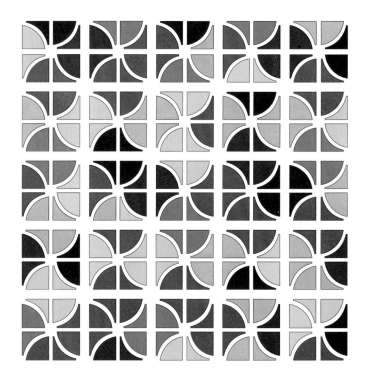

1. Working with one A and B set at a time, position the A shape on the B shape, right sides together with B extending 1/2" beyond A shape.

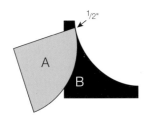

2. Hold one shape in each hand and slowly bring the curved edges together while stitching a 1/4" seam. Press seam toward A and press front and back of AB unit. Lay each sewn set back on the design wall after sewing to ensure placement stays consistent with design. Repeat with all A and B sets to make a total of (100) AB units.

Press seam →

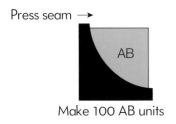

Make 100 AB units

SQUARING UP THE AB SHAPES

1. Square up the AB units to 4" squares. Position the QCRM on AB as shown, with the B piece at the top right position. Leave 1/8" from curved seam to outer edges. Trim right and top. Lift ruler, rotate block, reposition QCRM, aligning previously trimmed edges with the 4" marks on the ruler. Trim side and top. Repeat for all AB units.

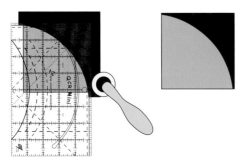

2. Reposition AB sets back on the design wall for consistent design.

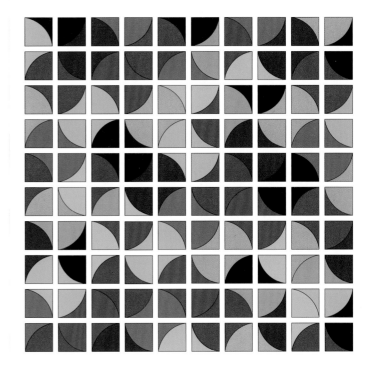

QUILT ASSEMBLY

1. Working with the first row on your design wall, sew AB units together to make 10 rows. Press seams open.

2. Sew all rows together to complete quilt top. Press seams open.

FINISHING THE QUILT

1. Layer the quilt top, batting and backing together. Quilt as desired.

2. Cut 2-1/2" strips from binding fabric and sew together, end to end, to make one long binding strip. Press seams open.

3. Press strip wrong sides together. Sew to front of quilt along raw edges. Fold binding to the back, covering raw edges, and hand stitch in place.

I see a *bad moon* a-rising
I see trouble on the way
I see earthquakes and
lightnin'
I see bad times today

—Creedence Clearwater Revival

Bat Moon Rising

Finished size: 31" x 52"

MATERIALS

(4) assorted black fat quarters. Designate assortment as black 1, black 2, black 3, and black 4.

(1) white fat quarter

2-¼ yards background fabric

1-¾ yards backing fabric

½ yard binding fabric

QCR Mini Ruler (QCRM)

GENERAL CUTTING INSTRUCTIONS

 From black 1 fat quarter, cut:

(6) 5-½" squares

    Cut squares in half diagonally.

 From black 2 fat quarter, cut:

(6) 5-½" squares

    Cut squares in half diagonally.

    Set aside 1 triangle.

 From black 3 fat quarter, cut:

(6) 5-½" squares

    Cut squares in half diagonally.

 From black 4 fat quarter, cut:

(5) 5-½" squares

    Cut squares in half diagonally.

    Set aside 1 triangle.

From white fabric, cut:

(4) 5" squares

(1) 4" square

 From background fabric, cut:

(7) 4" x WOF strips. From strips, cut:

    (61) 4" squares

(1) 5" x WOF strip. From strip, cut:

    (3) 5" squares

(4) 7-½" x WOF strips. From strips, cut:

    (22) 4-½" x 7-½" pieces

(5) 2" x WOF strips. Sew strips end-to-end and cut:

    (2) 2" x 31-½" strips

    (2) 2" x 49-½" strips

WOF = width of fabric

Read through Using the QCR Mini Ruler, pages 6-10 before beginning this project.

CUTTING WITH THE QCR MINI RULER

1. From the (4) 5" white squares, stack a few and align the adjoining sides along the dashed "V" lines on the QCRM ruler. Cut in the curved cutout (red dashed line) to make (4) A and (4) B shapes. Discard (1) B shape.

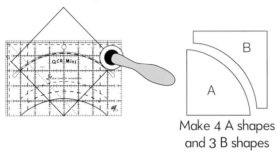

Make 4 A shapes
and 3 B shapes

2. From the (3) 5" background squares, stack a few and align the adjoining sides along the dashed "V" lines on the QCRM ruler. Cut in the curved cutout (red dashed line) to make (3) A and (3) B shapes.

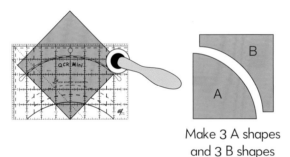

Make 3 A shapes
and 3 B shapes

3. From the 4-1/2" x 7-1/2" background pieces, stack a few, and align the adjoining sides along the dashed "V" lines on the QCRM ruler. Cut in the curved cutout to make A shapes. Repeat on the opposite diagonal corner as shown, for a total of (44) background A shapes. Discard (1) A shape or save for another project. Discard small pieces of fabric.

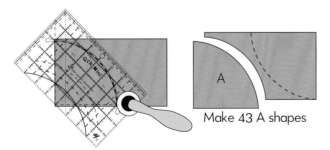

Make 43 A shapes

4. From bat 1 triangles, stack a few, measure and mark 1/2" on both points and trim as shown. Position the QCRM on the triangle with the curved cutout on the 1/2" marks. Cut in the curved cutout to make (12) B1 shapes. Discard small pieces of fabric.

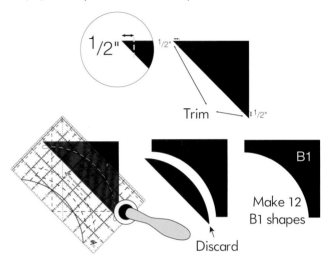

Trim

Make 12
B1 shapes

Discard

5. From bat 2 triangles, stack a few, measure and mark 1/2" on both points and trim as shown. Position the QCRM on the triangle with the curved cutout on the 1/2" marks. Cut in the curved cutout to make (11) B2 shapes. Discard small pieces of fabric.

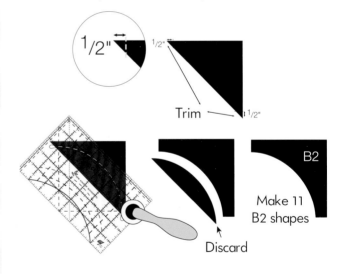

Trim

Make 11
B2 shapes

Discard

6. From bat 3 triangles, stack a few, measure and mark 1/2" on both points and trim as shown. Position the QCRM on the triangle with the curved cutout on the 1/2" marks. Cut in the curved cutout to make (12) B3 shapes. Discard small pieces of fabric.

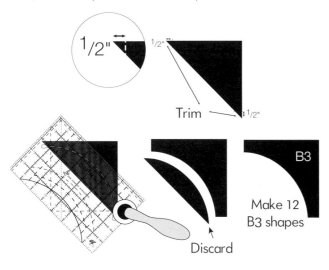

Trim

Make 12
B3 shapes

Discard

7. From bat 4 triangles, stack a few, measure and mark 1/2" on both points and trim as shown. Position the QCRM on the triangle with the curved cutout on the 1/2" marks. Cut in the curved cutout to make (9) B shapes. Discard small pieces of fabric.

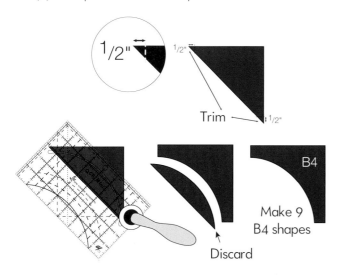

Trim

Make 9
B4 shapes

Discard

PIECING THE CURVES

1. Lay out the following sets:

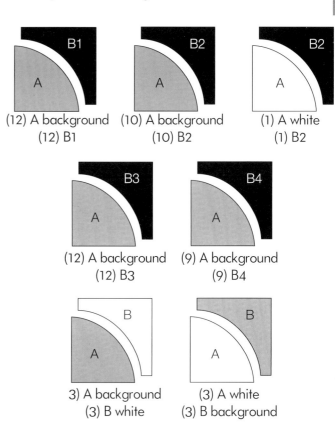

(12) A background
(12) B1

(10) A background
(10) B2

(1) A white
(1) B2

(12) A background
(12) B3

(9) A background
(9) B4

3) A background
(3) B white

(3) A white
(3) B background

2. Referring to the diagram, position an A shape on a B shape, right sides together, with B extending 1/2" beyond A. Hold one shape in each hand and slowly bring the curved edges together while stitching a 1/4" seam. Press seam toward A and press front and back of AB unit. Repeat for all A and B shapes in above sets.

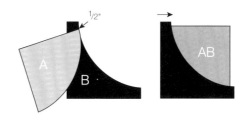

SQUARING UP THE AB UNITS

Square up the AB units to 4" squares. Position the QCRM on AB as shown, with the B piece at the top right position. Leave 1⁄8" from curved seam to outer edges. Trim right and top. Lift ruler, rotate block, reposition QCRM, aligning previously trimmed edges with the 4" marks on the ruler. Trim side and top. Repeat for all AB units.

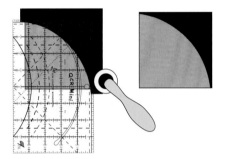

MAKING THE QUILT SECTIONS

Section 1

1. Lay out the following pieces:

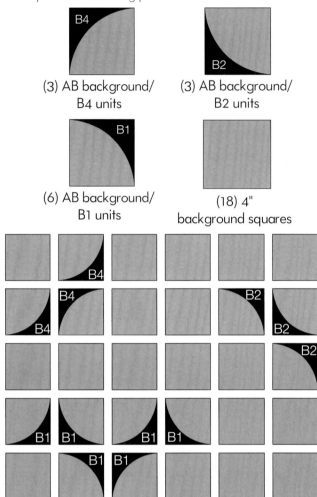

(3) AB background/ B4 units   (3) AB background/ B2 units

(6) AB background/ B1 units   (18) 4" background squares

2. Sew units together in rows. Press seams open. Sew rows together and press seams open to complete section 1.

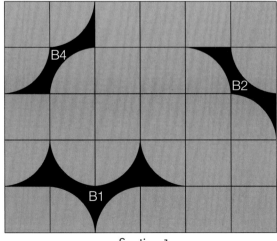

Section 1

Section 2

1. Lay out the following pieces:

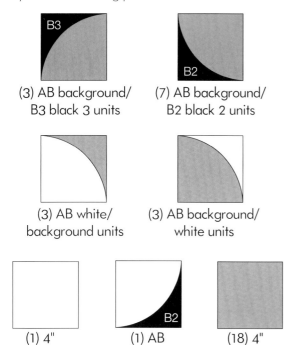

(3) AB background/
B3 black 3 units

(7) AB background/
B2 black 2 units

(3) AB white/
background units

(3) AB background/
white units

(1) 4"
white square

(1) AB
white/black
2 unit

(18) 4"
background
squares

2. Sew units together in rows. Press seams open. Sew rows together and press seams open to complete section 2.

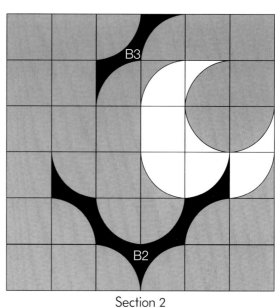

Section 2

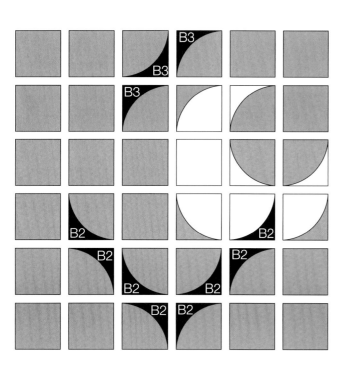

Section 3

1. Lay out the following pieces:

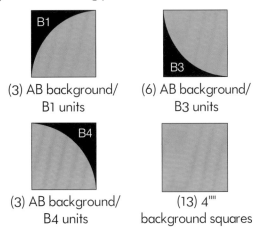

(3) AB background/
B1 units

(6) AB background/
B3 units

(3) AB background/
B4 units

(13) 4""
background squares

2. Sew units together in rows. Press seams open. Sew rows together and press seams open to complete section 3.

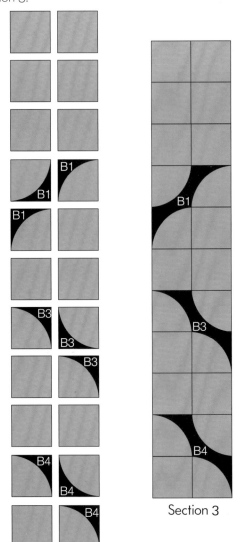

Section 3

Section 4

1. Lay out the following pieces:

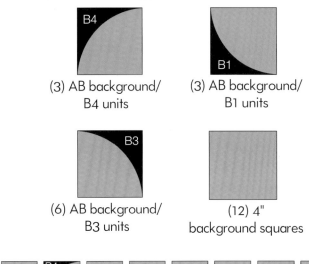

(3) AB background/
B4 units

(3) AB background/
B1 units

(6) AB background/
B3 units

(12) 4"
background squares

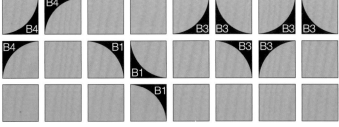

2. Sew units together in rows. Press seams open. Sew rows together and press seams open to complete section 4.

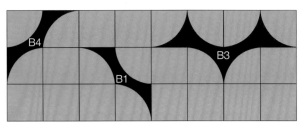

Section 4

QUILT TOP ASSEMBLY

1. With right sides together, sew section 1 to section 2, matching seams. Press seams open.

2. With right sides together, sew section 3 to section 1/2, matching seams. Press seams open.

3. With right sides together, sew section 1/2/3, to section 4, matching seams. Press seams open.

4. Sew 2" x 49-1/2" borders to each side of quilt. Press seams toward border.

5. Sew 2" x 31-1/2" borders to top and bottom of quilt. Press seams toward border.

FINISHING THE QUILT

1. Layer the quilt top, batting and backing together. Quilt as desired.

2. Cut 2-1/2" strips from binding fabric and sew together, end to end, to make one long binding strip. Press seams open.

3. Press strip wrong sides together. Sew to front of quilt along raw edges. Fold binding to the back, covering raw edges, and hand stitch in place.

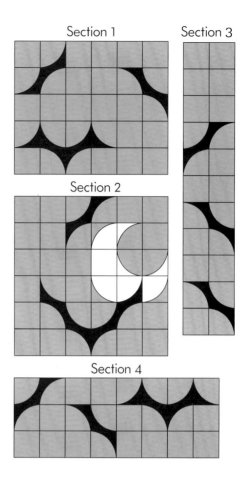

Section 1

Section 3

Section 2

Section 4

"*Listen!*
The wind is rising,
and the air is wild
with leaves,

We have had our summer
evenings, now for
October eves!"
— Humbert Wolfe

October Eves

Finished size: 35" x 35"

MATERIALS

(18) 10" assorted orange and
    yellow squares
(4) assorted purple hue fat quarters
    for background
1-¼ backing fabric
⅓ yard binding fabric
QCR Mini Ruler (QCRM)

GENERAL CUTTING INSTRUCTIONS

 **From (1) 10" assorted square, cut:**
(4) 1" x 10" strips for stems

 **From *each* of (17) 10" assorted squares, cut:**
(4) 5" squares for a total of 68

 **From EACH purple fat quarter,
following the cutting diagram, cut:**
(1) 8" square
(4) 4" squares
(4) 4-½" x 7-½" pieces

4½" x 7½"	4½" x 7½"	4½" x 7½"	4½" x 7½"
4" x 4"	4" x 4"		
4" x 4"	4" x 4"	8" x 8"	

WOF = width of fabric
Read through Using the QCR Mini Ruler,
pages 6-10 before beginning this project.

CUTTING WITH THE QCR MINI RULER

1. Separate the 5" squares into (2) stacks, with
    (56) assorted squares in Stack 1, and (12) squares
    in Stack 2. Be sure to mix the fabrics well as you
    separate squares into stacks.

Stack 1
56 squares

Stack 2
12 squares

2. Working with Stack 1, stack a few and align the
    adjoining sides along the dashed "V" lines on the
    QCRM ruler. Cut in the curved cutout (yellow dashed
    line) to make A and B shapes. Repeat with all squares
    in Stack 1 for a total of (56) A and B shapes. Select
    (24) A shapes, setting aside (32) A shapes for another
    project. Keep all B shapes.

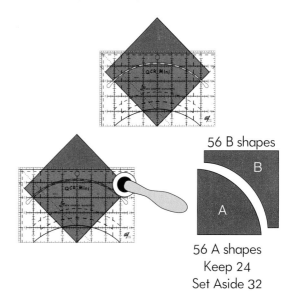

56 B shapes

56 A shapes
Keep 24
Set Aside 32

3. From the 4-1/2" x 7-1/2" purple pieces, stack a few, and align the adjoining sides along the dashed "V" lines on the QCRM ruler. Cut in the curved cutout to make A shapes. Repeat on the opposite diagonal corner as shown, for a total of (32) purple A shapes, (8) from each purple hue. Discard small pieces of fabric.

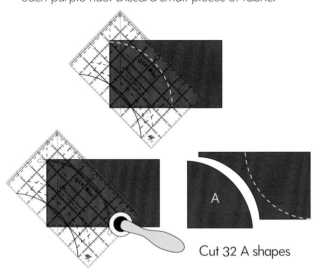

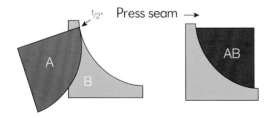

Cut 32 A shapes

PIECING THE CURVES

Sew the following sets together:

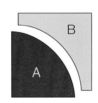

24 assorted orange/ yellow A and B shapes

32 purple A shapes and 32 assorted orange/ yellow B shapes

1. Referring to the diagram, position an A shape on a B shape, right sides together, with B extending 1/2" beyond A. Hold one shape in each hand and slowly bring the curved edges together while stitching a 1/4" seam. Press seam toward A and press front and back of AB shape.

1/2" → Press seam →

2. Repeat for all A and B sets to make (24) assorted orange/yellow AB units and (32) assorted orange/yellow/purple AB units.

24 assorted orange/ yellow AB units

32 assorted purple/ orange/yellow AB units

SQUARING UP THE AB SHAPES

Square up the AB units to 4" squares. Position the QCRM on AB as shown, with the B piece at the top right position. Leave an 1/8" from curved seam to outer edges. Trim right and top. Lift ruler, rotate block, reposition QCRM, aligning previously trimmed edges with the 4" marks on the ruler. Trim side and top. Repeat for all AB units.

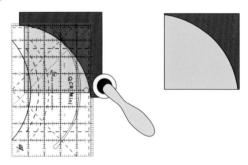

PIECING HALF SQUARE TRIANGLES

1. Using stack 2 squares, draw a diagonal line on 6 of the remaining 5" orange/yellow squares as shown.

2. Layer a marked square on an unmarked 5" assorted orange/yellow square, right sides together. Sew 1/4" on both sides of the drawn line. Cut on the drawn line. Press open to make (2) half-square triangles.

3. Repeat with remaining 5" orange/yellow squares for a total of 12 half-square triangles. Square the units to 4" squares.

MAKING THE LEAF STEMS

1. Draw a diagonal line on an 8" purple square and cut on drawn line.

2. With right sides together, center a 1" x 10" stem on the diagonal cut, aligning edges. Sew stem to triangle and press seams toward stem.

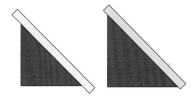

3. With right sides together, center the remaining triangle on the stem. Sew to stem and press seams towards stem.

4. Square up the unit to 7-1/2" squares. Repeat with remaining 8" purple squares to make a total of (4) stem, half-square triangle blocks.

MAKING THE LEAF BLOCKS

1. Lay out 6 orange/yellow AB shapes, 8 purple/ orange/yellow AB shapes, 3 orange/yellow half-square triangles, 4 purple squares, and a stem section, matching purple hues throughout.

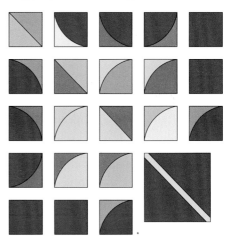

2. Sew units in rows, press seams open, and sew rows together to make an 18" leaf block. Press seams open to reduce bulk.

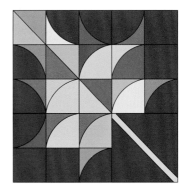

3. Repeat steps 1 and 2 to make 4 leaf blocks, making sure to match purple hues in each block.

ASSEMBLING THE QUILT TOP

Lay out the 4 leaf blocks as shown. Sew blocks together to complete top. Press seams open.

FINISHING THE QUILT

1. Layer the quilt top, batting and backing together. Quilt as desired.

2. Cut 2-1/2" strips from binding fabric and sew together, end to end, to make one long binding strip. Press seams open.

3. Press strip wrong sides together. Sew to front of quilt along raw edges. Fold binding to the back, covering raw edges, and hand stitch in place.

"One of his tears fell in my mouth, where it became a blue sapphire, source of *strength,* and *eternal hope.*"

— Anita Diamant

Winter Jewels

Finished size: 17" x 48"

MATERIALS

(12) Fat quarters of assorted prints.
  Select prints in 3 sets of 4
  that work well together.
1/2 yard fabric for background,
  sashing and borders
1-1/2 yard backing fabric
1/2 yard binding fabric
QCR Mini Ruler (QCRM)

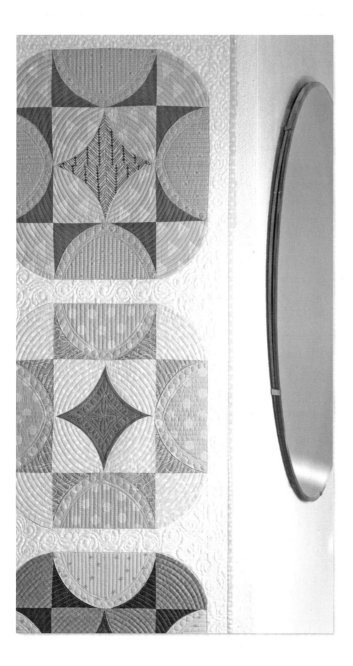

GENERAL CUTTING INSTRUCTIONS

Working with block diagram and only one set of (4) fat quarters, decide which fabric will be 1, 2, 3 and 4.

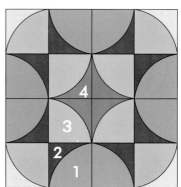

 From color 1, cut:
(4) 4-1/2" x 7-1/2" pieces

 From color 2, cut:
(4) 5-1/2" squares. Cut squares in half diagonally for a total of 8 triangles.

 From color 3, cut:
(4) 4-1/2" x 7-1/2" pieces

 From color 4, cut:
(2) 5-1/2" squares. Cut squares in half diagonally for a total of 4 triangles.

Follow cutting instructions above for each Winter Jewel block set.

 From solid fabric, cut:
(1) 5-1/2" x WOF strip. From the strip cut:
  (6) 5-1/2" squares. Cut squares in half
  diagonally for a total of 12 triangles.
(4) 2" x WOF strips. Sew strips end-to-end
  and cut:
  (2) 2" x 48-1/2" strips
  (4) 2" x 14-1/2" strips

WOF = width of fabric
Read through Using the QCR Mini Ruler, pages 6-10 before beginning this project.

CUTTING WITH THE QCR MINI RULER

1. Working with one Winter Jewel block fabric set at a time, stack a few 4-½" x 7-½" pieces from colors 1 and 3 and align the adjoining sides along the dashed "V" lines on the QCRM ruler. Cut in the curved cutout to make A shapes. Repeat on the opposite diagonal corner as shown, for a total of (16) A shapes. Repeat for each additional block set. Discard small pieces of fabric.

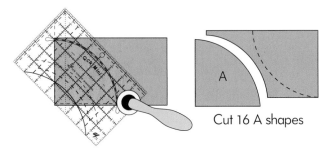

Cut 16 A shapes

2. From the 5-½" color 2 and 4 triangles, stack a few and measure in ½" on each diagonal point and trim as shown. Position the QCRM on the triangle with the curved cutout on the ½" marks. Cut in the curved cutout to make a total of (12) B shapes. Discard small pieces of fabric. Repeat for each additional block set.

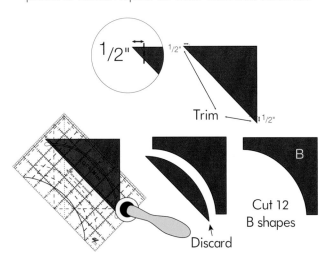

Trim

Cut 12 B shapes

Discard

3. From background fabric triangles, repeat step 2 to make (12) B shapes.

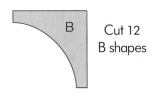

Cut 12 B shapes

PIECING THE CURVES

1. Working with one block set, lay out the following:

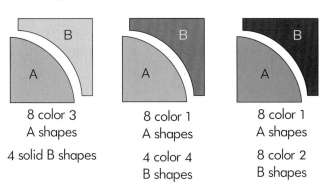

8 color 3 A shapes

4 solid B shapes

8 color 1 A shapes

4 color 4 B shapes

8 color 1 A shapes

8 color 2 B shapes

2. Working with one set at a time, and referring to the diagram, position an A shape on a B shape, right sides together, with B extending ½" beyond A. Hold one shape in each hand and slowly bring the curved edges together while stitching a ¼" seam. Press seam toward A and press front and back of AB unit.

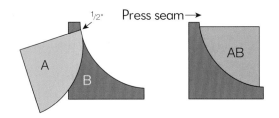

½"   Press seam →

A   B   AB

3. Repeat layout and step 1 for additional block sets. There will be a total of (16) AB units for each block.

SQUARING UP THE AB UNITS

Square up the AB units to 4" squares. Position the QCRM on AB as shown, with the B piece at the top right position. Leave ⅛" from curved seam to outer edges. Trim right and top. Lift ruler, rotate block, reposition QCRM, aligning previously trimmed edges with the 4" marks on the ruler. Trim side and top. Repeat for all AB units.

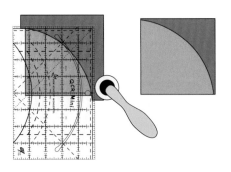

BLOCK ASSEMBLY

1. Lay out each Winter Jewels block as shown. Sew units together in rows. Press seams open. Sew rows together to complete center block. Press seams open.

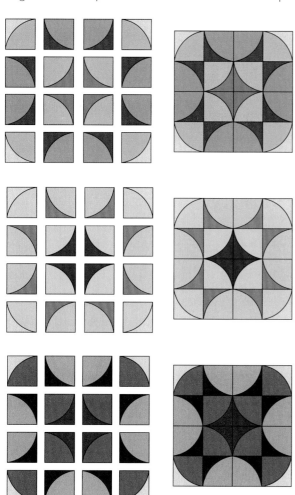

2. Lay out blocks and 2" x 14-1/2" sashing as shown. Sew sashing between blocks and on top and bottom. Press seams toward sashing.

3. Sew 2" x 48-1/2" borders to each side of runner. Press seams toward borders.

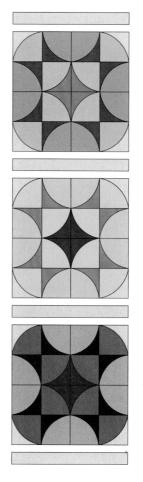

FINISHING THE QUILT

1. Layer the quilt top, batting and backing together. Quilt as desired.

2. Cut 2-1/2" strips from binding fabric and sew together, end to end, to make one long binding strip. Press seams open.

3. Press strip wrong sides together. Sew to front of quilt along raw edges. Fold binding to the back, covering raw edges, and hand stitch in place.

Shall I compare thee to a *summer's day?*
Thou art more *lovely* and more temperate:
Rough winds do shake the darling buds of *May,*
And summer's lease hath all too short a date.

—William Shakespeare "Sonnet 18"

Breezy Day

Finished size: 42" x 42"

MATERIALS

(5) Assorted aqua fat quarters
(1) Pink fat quarter
2 yards background fabric
1-¾ yards backing fabric
½ yard binding fabric
QCR Mini Ruler (QCRM)

GENERAL CUTTING INSTRUCTIONS

 From each assorted aqua fat quarter, cut:
(8) 5" squares for a total of 40 squares

 **From one of the aqua fat quarters,
cut an additional**
(4) 5" squares, for a total of (44) 5" aqua squares

 From pink fabric, cut:
(64) 1-¾" squares

 From background fabric, cut:
(6) 5" x WOF strips. From the strips, cut:
  (44) 5" squares
(6) 4" x WOF strips. From the strips, cut:
  (56) 4" squares

WOF = width of fabric
Read through Using the QCR Mini Ruler,
pages 6-10 before beginning this project.

CUTTING WITH THE QCR MINI RULER

1. From the (44) 5" assorted aqua squares, stack a few and align the adjoining sides along the dashed "V" lines on the QCRM ruler. Cut in the curved cutout (red dashed line) to make a total of (44) A and B shapes.

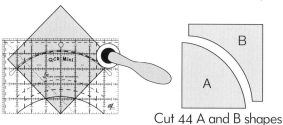

Cut 44 A and B shapes

2. From the (44) 5" background squares, stack a few and align the adjoining sides along the dashed "V" lines on the QCRM ruler. Cut in the curved cutout (red dashed line) to make a total of (44) A and B shapes.

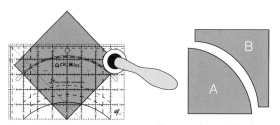

Cut 44 A and B shapes

PIECING THE CURVES

1. Referring to the diagram, position an A shape on a B shape, right sides together, with B extending ½" beyond A. Hold one shape in each hand and slowly bring the curved edges together while stitching a ¼" seam. Press seam toward A and press front and back of AB unit.

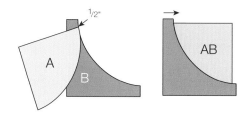

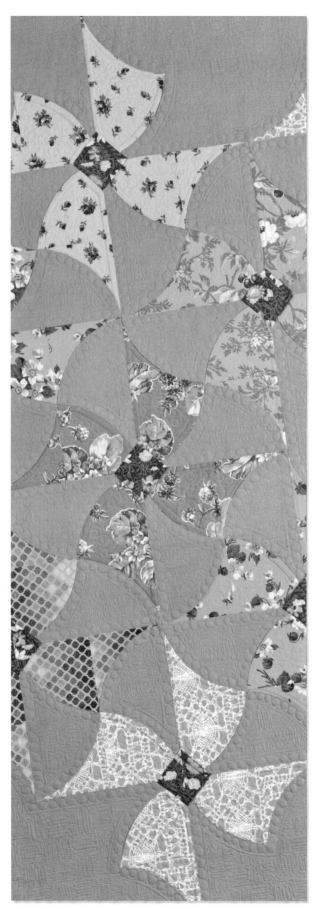

2. Repeat with all A and B shapes to make (44) aqua/
   background AB units and (44) background/aqua
   AB units.

Make 44 aqua/   Make 44 background/
background AB units   aqua AB units

SQUARING UP THE AB SHAPES

Square up the AB units to 4" squares. Position the
QCRM on AB as shown, with the B piece at the top
right position. Leave an 1/8" from curved seam to outer
edges. Trim right and top. Lift ruler, rotate block,
reposition QCRM, aligning previously trimmed edges
with the 4" marks on the ruler. Trim side and top.
Repeat for all AB units.

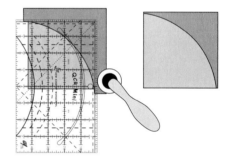

DIAMONDS AND PINWHEEL CENTERS

1. Draw a diagonal line on the wrong side of the 1-3/4"
   pink squares. Position a marked pink square on the
   corner of a 4" background square. Sew on the drawn
   line. Trim the corner 1/4" from sewn line. Press seam
   open. Repeat to make a total of (20) 4" background/
   pink squares.

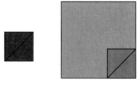

Make 20
background/pink
AB squares

2. Repeat step 1 to make (44) aqua/background AB units. Sew a pink square on same corners of each AB unit as shown.

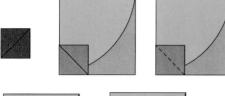

Make 44 aqua/ background/pink AB squares

QUILT ASSEMBLY

1. Lay out AB units in four sections, matching aqua fabric in each pinwheel as shown.

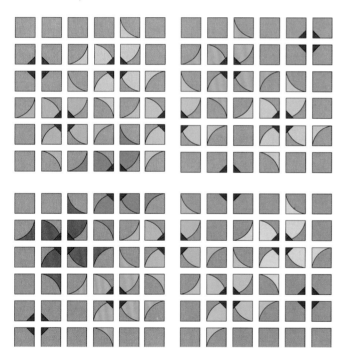

2. Sew units together in rows. Press seams open. Sew rows together to make a section. Press seams open.

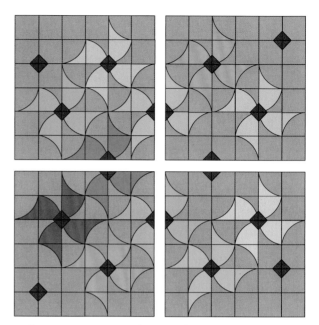

3. Sew 4 sections together matching seams. Press seams open.

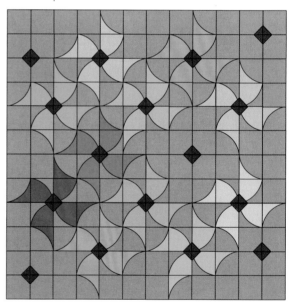

FINISHING THE QUILT

1. Layer the quilt top, batting and backing together. Quilt as desired.

2. Cut 2-1/2" strips from binding fabric and sew together, end to end, to make one long binding strip. Press seams open.

3. Press strip wrong sides together. Sew to front of quilt along raw edges. Fold binding to the back, covering raw edges, and hand stitch in place.

"No my friend,
darkness is not
everywhere,
for here and
there I find faces
illuminated
from within; paper
lanterns
among the
dark trees."

— Carole Borges

Lanterns

Finished size: 28" x 51"

MATERIALS

(6) Fat quarters of assorted prints
1 yard background fabric
1-¾ yards backing fabric
½ yard binding fabric
QCR Mini Ruler (QCRM)

GENERAL CUTTING INSTRUCTIONS

 From each fat quarter, cut:
(1) 7-½" square for a total of 6
(4) 5" squares for a total of 24
(2) 2" x 7-½" pieces for a total of 12

From background fabric, cut:
(3) 5-½" x WOF strips. From strips, cut:
   (24) 4" x 5-½" pieces
(3) 5" x WOF strips. From strips, cut:
   (24) 5" squares

WOF = width of fabric
Read through Using the QCR Mini Ruler,
pages 6-10 before beginning this project.

CUTTING WITH THE QCR MINI RULER

1. From the 5" assorted print squares and background
    squares, stack a few and align the adjoining sides
    along the dashed "V" lines on the QCRM ruler. Cut in
    the curved cutout (red dashed line) to make A and B
    shapes. Repeat for all assorted print and background
    squares for a total of (24) A and B print shapes and
    (24) background A and B shapes.

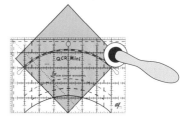

Cut 24 A and
B print shapes

Cut 24 A and B
background shapes

PIECING THE CURVES

1. Lay out A and B shapes in sets:

24 A print shapes and   24 A background shapes
24 B background shapes   and 24 B print shapes

2. Referring to the diagram, position an A shape on a B shape, right sides together, with B extending ½" beyond A. Hold one shape in each hand and slowly bring the curved edges together while stitching a ¼" seam. Press seam toward A and press front and back of AB unit. Repeat with sets to make (24) AB print/background units and(24) AB background/print units.

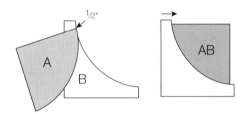

SQUARING UP THE AB UNITS

Square up the AB units to 4" squares. Position the QCRM on AB as shown, with the B piece at the top right position. Leave ⅛" from curved seam to outer edges. Trim right and top. Lift ruler, rotate block, reposition QCRM, aligning previously trimmed edges with the 4" marks on the ruler. Trim side and top. Repeat for all AB units.

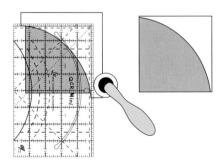

LANTERN BLOCK ASSEMBLY

1. Lay out one lantern block as shown, matching the fabric in AB units. Sew units together. Use contrasting fabrics for 7-½" center square and 2" x 7-½" strips.

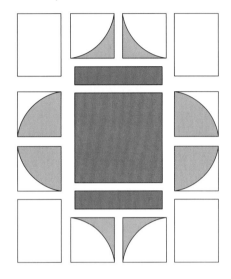

2. Sew a 2" x 7-½" strip to the AB units as shown in the layout diagram. Sew a 4" x 5-½" background piece to each side of the AB/strip unit. Sew lantern unit together in three rows, and press seams open.

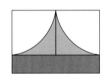

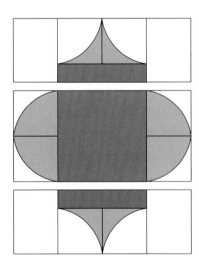

3. Sew rows together to finish lantern block. Press seams open. Repeat to make (6) lantern blocks.

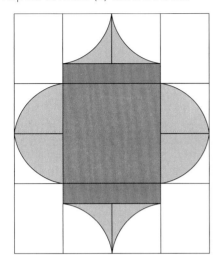

QUILT ASSEMBLY

1. Layout lantern blocks in rows of two.

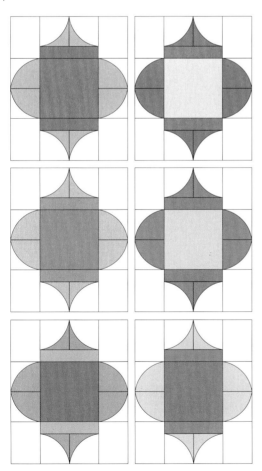

2. Sew rows together and press seams open. Sew rows together to finish quilt top. Press seams open.

FINISHING THE QUILT

1. Layer the quilt top, batting and backing together. Quilt as desired.

2. Cut 2-½" strips from binding fabric and sew together, end to end, to make one long binding strip. Press seams open.

3. Press strip wrong sides together. Sew to front of quilt along raw edges. Fold binding to the back, covering raw edges, and hand stitch in place.

Giving Tree

Finished size: 28" x 35"

MATERIALS

(4) Fat quarters of assorted green fabrics
(2) 5-½" gold squares for star
(1) 5" brown square for trunk
1 yard background fabric
1-¼yard backing fabric
⅓ yard binding fabric
QCR Mini Ruler (QCRM)

GENERAL CUTTING INSTRUCTIONS

From each assorted green fabric, cut:
(10) 5" squares for a total of 40,
    set aside (2)

From gold fabric, cut:
(2) 5-½" squares. Cut in half diagonally.

From 5" brown square, cut:
(2) 2-½" x 5" pieces

From background fabric, cut:
(1) 11" x WOF strip. From the strip, cut:
    (2) 11" squares
    (2) 4" x 11 pieces
(2) 7-½" x WOF strips. From the strips, cut:
    (2) 7-½" squares
    (2) 4" x 7-½" pieces
    (9) 4-½" x 7-½" pieces
(1) 2-½" x WOF strip. From the strip, cut:
    (2) 2-½" x 5" pieces

WOF = width of fabric
Read through Using the QCR Mini Ruler,
pages 6-10 before beginning this project.

TREE TRUNK ASSEMBLY

1. With right sides together, sew a 2-½" x 5" brown piece to a 2-½" x 5" background piece to make one half of trunk unit. Press seams open. Square unit to 4".

2. Repeat step one to make a second trunk unit. Square up unit to 4". Sew units together, brown to brown, to make tree trunk.

CUTTING WITH THE QUICK CURVE MINI RULER

1. From the (38) 5" assorted green squares, stack a few and align the adjoining sides along the dashed "V" lines on the QCRM ruler. Cut in the curved cutout (red dashed line) to make A and B shapes. Repeat for all assorted green print squares. Select (24) A shapes and (38) B shapes for tree boughs. This is to ensure variety to create AB units. Keep extra A shapes for another project.

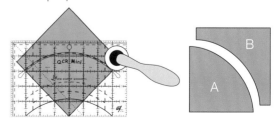

Cut 38 A and 38 B shapes
Select 24 A shapes and 38 B shapes

2. From the 5-½" star triangles, stack a few and measure in ½" on each diagonal point and trim as shown. Position the QCRM on the triangle with the curved cutout on the ½" marks. Cut in the curved cutout to make a total of (4) B shapes.

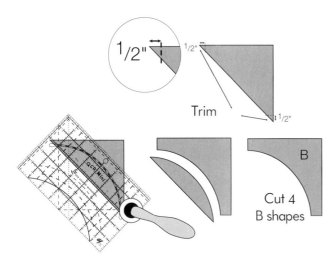

Trim

B

Cut 4
B shapes

3. From the (9) 4-½" x 7-½" background pieces, stack a few, and align the adjoining sides along the dashed "V" lines on the QCRM ruler. Cut in the curved cutout to make A shapes. Repeat on the opposite diagonal corner as shown, for a total of (18) A shapes. Discard small pieces of fabric.

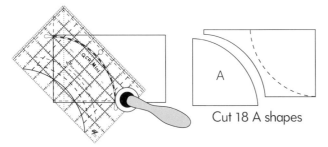

A

Cut 18 A shapes

PIECING THE CURVES

NOTE: This is a "design wall" quilt. Lay out the A and B shapes on your wall as shown in the diagram.

On a design wall, lay out A and B shapes, trunk unit, and background pieces to create the tree. Sew A and B shapes together, 1 set at a time and lay each sewn set back on design wall to ensure placement stays consistent with design.

PIECING THE CURVES

Referring to the diagram, position an A shape on a background B shape, right sides together, with B extending ½" beyond A. Hold one shape in each hand and slowly bring the curved edges together while stitching a ¼" seam. Press seam toward A and press front and back of AB unit. Repeat for all sets to make (4) AB units for star and (38) AB units for tree.

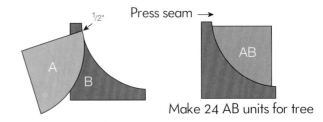

Press seam →

A

B

AB

Make 24 AB units for tree

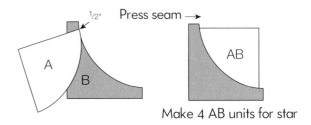

Press seam →

A

B

AB

Make 4 AB units for star

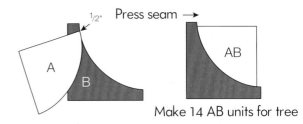

Press seam →

A

B

AB

Make 14 AB units for tree

SQUARING UP THE AB SHAPES

1. Square up the AB units to 4" squares. Position the QCRM on AB as shown, with the B piece at the top right position. Leave 1/8" from curved seam to outer edges. Trim right and top. Lift ruler, rotate block, reposition QCRM, aligning previously trimmed edges with the 4" marks on the ruler. Trim side and top. Repeat for all AB units.

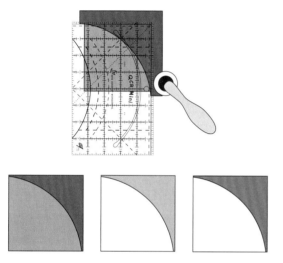

2. Reposition AB sets back on the design wall for consistent design.

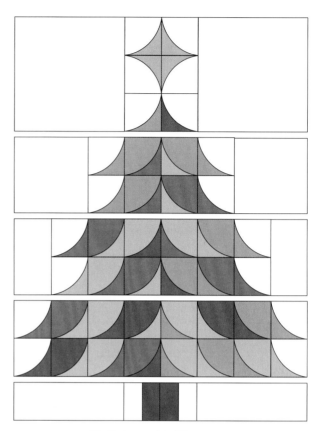

Quilt Assembly Diagram

QUILT ASSEMBLY

1. From your design wall, start at the top of the tree to create rows as shown in the Quilt Assembly Diagram. Press seams open.

2. Sew rows together to finish tree quilt. Press seams open.

FINISHING THE QUILT

1. Layer the quilt top, batting and backing together. Quilt as desired.

2. Cut 2-1/2" strips from binding fabric and sew together, end to end, to make one long binding strip. Press seams open.

3. Press strip wrong sides together. Sew to front of quilt along raw edges. Fold binding to the back, covering raw edges, and hand stitch in place.

Quilting Suggestions

Early Risers

Color Love

Heart Beat

Bird Song

Quilting Suggestions

Spring Wings

Sea Glass

Soak Up The Sun

Freedom's Flag

#arewethereyet

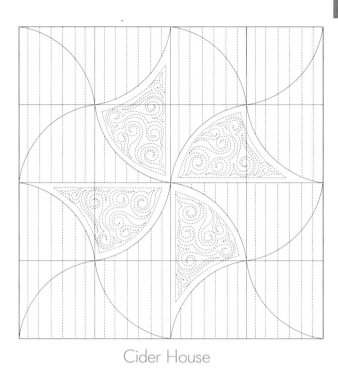

Cider House

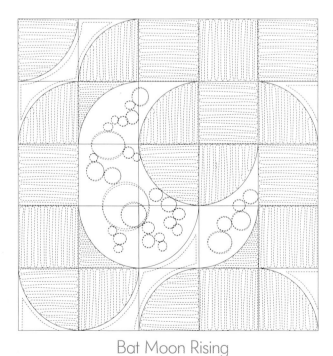

Bat Moon Rising

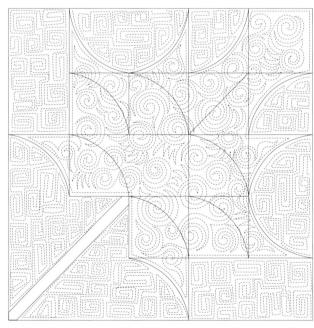

October Eves

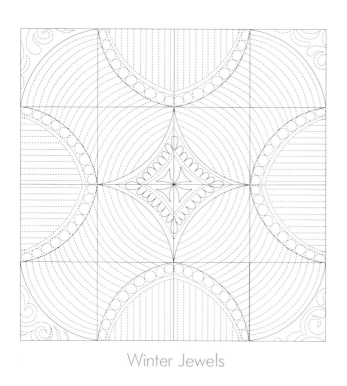

Winter Jewels

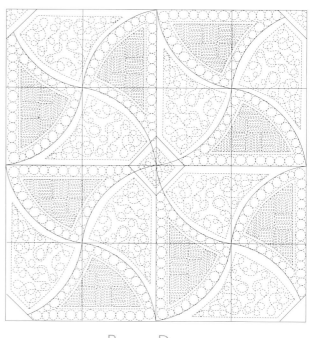

Breezy Day

Lanterns

Giving Tree